BACKGROUND TO MORALITY

Thomas J. Harte, C.SS.R., Ph.D

Louis F. Hartman, C.SS.R., S.S.L

William F. Jenks, C.SS.R., Ph.D

James Kerins, C.SS.R., Ph.D

Daniel Lowery, C.SS.R., Ph.D

Francis X. Murphy, C.SS.R., Ph.D

Henry V. Sattler, C.SS.R., Ph.D

BACKGROUND
TO MORALITY ▸▸

edited by *John P. Lerhinan,* C.SS.R.

88565

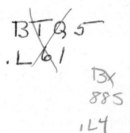

DESCLEE COMPANY

New York   Tournai   Paris   Rome

BTQ 5 .L61   ST. JOSEPH'S UNIVERSITY   STX

Background to morality,

3 9353 00006 3345

The scriptural quotations in this book are reproduced by license of Confraternity of Christian Doctrine, Washington, D.C. Used with permission. All rights reserved.

IMPRIMI POTEST
Ronald Connors, C.SS.R.
Provincial Superior
October 24, 1964

NIHIL OBSTAT
James F. Rigney, S.T.D.
Censor Librorum

IMPRIMATUR
✠*Francis Cardinal Spellman*
Archbishop of New York
November 5, 1964

The nihil obstat and imprimatur are official declarations that a book or pamphlet is free of doctrinal or moral error. No implication is contained therein that those who have granted the nihil obstat and imprimatur agree with the contents, opinions or statements expressed.

© 1964 by Desclee Co., Inc.
Printed in the United States of America by H. Wolff, New York

Preface

▶▶

This collection of essays on religious and social questions is presented as a tribute to Father Francis Connell on the occasion of his Golden Jubilee as a priest.

All of the writers are members of the Redemptorist Community at Holy Redeemer College, Washington, D.C., where Father Connell resides. All of them have been taught theology by Father Connell either at Mount St. Alphonsus, Esopus, N.Y., where he was professor of dogmatic theology from 1915 to 1921 and again from 1924 to 1940, or at the Catholic University of America where he lectured in Moral Theology from 1940 to 1958.

We learned from Father Connell the importance of an intensive and continuing study of theology and its related branches. We also learned to combine a loyalty to the official decisions of the Church with an awareness of the many questions that are open for discussion and further investigation. We learned, further, that one should defend courageously those opinions—whether old or new—which he judges to be true.

Human knowledge is always incomplete and each generation has its contribution to make. Father Connell surely has made his. His example challenges us to make ours.

Very Reverend John Lerhinan, C.SS.R., Ph.D.

Contents

▶▶

BACKGROUND TO MORALITY

Salvation History
of the Old Testament
▶▶

LOUIS F. HARTMAN, C.SS.R., S.S.L., Ling. Orient. Lic.

The Nature of Salvation History

It is quite obvious that the Sacred Scriptures are primarily concerned with God's dealings with man, and more particularly with the carrying out of God's plan for man's ultimate happiness. In a certain sense, therefore, all readers of the Bible throughout the centuries were more or less aware of the fact that biblical history is the history of man's salvation. But it was only in the 19th century that this idea was first stressed and made the basis in biblical theology for a deeper understanding of the divine revelation that is contained in the Sacred Scriptures. Since this particular theological aspect of biblical history originated in Germany, even scholars writing in English often refer to it by the German term, *Heilsgeschichte*. The equivalent English term is "salvation history." But we cannot form an English adjective from this term in the way one can speak in German of a *"heilsgechichtlich* event."

Two factors in the mentality of the Israelites contributed to the fact that God revealed Himself to them in the form of salvation history. On the one hand, Israelite thinking was what has been well called "dynamic." Not only did the Israelites prefer concrete images to abstract ideas, as did all the other peoples of the ancient Near East; they were also more interested in acts and events than in the nature and existence of things. Providentially they were thus disposed by nature to be historically minded. In this respect they were rather unique among the various peoples of the ancient Near East. They were, in fact, the only people who wrote genuine history, albeit history of a special kind, five centuries before the classical historians of ancient Greece. On the other hand, the Israelites were like all other peoples of the ancient Near East in that their mentality was essentially religious. They made no clear-cut distinction between the religious and the profane. For them, all that happened in the world of nature and of man was the direct result of the divine forces that were active in the world. But whereas the surrounding pagan nations, with their more "static" mentality, thought of the divine forces in the world as personal gods and goddesses who, after their first victory over the powers of chaos, ruled the world in an unchanging cycle of natural seasons and ever-recurring vicissitudes in the affairs of men, Israel, with its dynamic mentality and under the influence of the revelation that God gave it, regarded these forces in nature and in history as manifestations of a single Creator, Israel's God, Yahweh, who is master of all His creation and who can therefore, at will both intervene in nature by working miracles and intervene in human history by the power of His *rûah* (originally "wind" and "breath," and then "spirit") working on man's *rûah* or spirit. For Israel, Yahweh is essentially "a God who acts."

That Israel regarded its religious history as "salvation" history was also determined by two basic considerations. First of all, there was the obvious fact that all was not right with the world. The Israelites, both as individuals and as a nation, were not always enjoying ideal happiness. In fact, most of the time they were suffering troubles of one sort or another, from which they longed to be delivered. At the same time, however, they were convinced that their God was an infinitely good God. Since Yahweh had called them to Himself and made them His "Chosen People," they expected Him to save them from their troubles. Their past salvation history, inasmuch as they could rightly regard themselves as "a people saved by Yahweh" (Dt 33,29), led them to a certain *Heilserwartung*, a certain hope and expectation that Yahweh would continue to bring them salvation in the future. And this confidence was not groundless; they had Yahweh's word for it: "I know well the plans I have in mind for you, says Yahweh, plans for your welfare, not for woe! plans to give you a future full of hope" (Jer 29,11). Throughout their history the Israelites called Yahweh their "saving God" (Is 17,10; Ps 67 [68], 20 etc.) and their "saving Rock" (Dt 32,15), that is, the impregnable fortress to which they fled for safety.

Early Salvation History

Modern biblical scholars rightly place Israel's awareness of its salvation history in the Mosaic period. The historical event of prime importance which led the Israelites to

believe in Yahweh as their saving God was the great
deliverance which He won for them by freeing them from
Egyptian bondage and rescuing them from Pharao's army.
"When Yahweh saved Israel from the hand of the Egyp-
tians" (Ex 14,30), Israel sang, "My strength and courage
is Yahweh, and he has been my savior" (Ex 15,2). The
memory of the miraculous Exodus from Egypt was always
to remain a vital force in Israel. When the Israelites are
urged to treat their slaves kindly, they are told, "Remember that you too were once slaves in Egypt, and Yahweh,
your God, brought you from there with his strong hand
and outstretched arm" (Dt 5,15). The salvation which
the Lord then wrought for Israel serves, in fact, as a motive
for keeping all of His commandments (Dt 6,20-23) in
loyalty to Him (Jos 24,16-17).

So also, the prophets harked back to the Exodus when
they pleaded for fidelity to Yahweh. "Did I not bring the
Israelites from the land of Egypt?" (Am 9,7). "I, Yahweh,
am your God since the land of Egypt; you know no God
besides me, and there is no savior but me" (Os 13,4).
"When Israel was a child I loved him; out of Egypt I
called my son" (Os 11,1). "O my people, what have I
done to you, or how have I wearied you? Answer me!
For I brought you up from the land of Egypt, from the
place of slavery I released you" (Mi 6,3-4). It was precisely
at that time that Yahweh showed Himself the mighty
conqueror of Israel's foes (Nm 23,21-22; 24,8).

This basic salvific event of the Exodus led Israel to view
its pre-Mosaic history also as salvation history, as far back,
in fact, as the time when Abraham's ancestors were still
polytheists (Jos 24,2-7). The great covenant which Yah-

weh made with Israel almost immediately after the Exodus
(Ex 24,1-8; 34,10-28) was regarded as foreshadowed in
the covenant which God made with Abraham (Gn 15;
18). The Israelites conquest of Chanaan, which in itself
was an act of salvation wrought by Yahweh, was viewed
as the fulfillment of the promises that God had made to
the patriarchs (Dt 6,18.23).

Even in the countless centuries "before Abraham was"
(Jn 8,58), of which Israel had no real historical memory,
salvation history was seen as already operative. The Yahwistic author, who wrote at about the time of David or
Solomon and whose work forms the major portion of
the book of Genesis, recorded not only the ancient traditions which had been orally handed down concerning
Israel's first forefathers, Abraham, Isaac, and Jacob, but
also the legendary stories which these men had brought
with them from Mesopotamia, such as the story of the
Deluge and the story of the Tower of Babel (Gn 6-8;
11,1-9). But now these ancient tales are interpreted by the
Yahwist as incidents in Israel's salvation history—as proof
of the ever-deepening moral corruption of mankind from
which God first rescued Noe (with whom He also made
a covenant!) and from which God later *called* Abraham
(the salvation-history theme of the call and the election):
"Leave your country, your kinsfolk and your father's
house, for the land which I will show you; I will make a
great nation of you. I will bless you, and make your name
great . . . In you shall all the nations of the earth be
blessed" (Gn 12,1-3).

The same Yahwistic writer begins his account with the
story of paradise and the fall of man (Gn 2,4b-3,24), in

which he not only strikes the keynote of all salvation history, the theme of human guilt and God's grace, but also indicates the basic reason why man needs God's salvation, even though the first one to realize the full import of the Yahwist's inspired insight into primeval guilt was the great theologian of the New Testament, Paul of Tarsus (Rom 5,12-19).

Closely connected with Israel's Exodus-experience of Yahweh as Israel's saving God was the solemn covenant which He made with this people at Mount Sinai, whereby Israel acknowledged Yahweh as its only God, and Yahweh took Israel to Himself as His "special possession," His Chosen People, guaranteeing to "save" them and bring them *salôm* (peace, happiness, and prosperity), as long as they kept the terms of His covenant, His moral law.

Other early national victories of Israel were likewise regarded as acts of "salvation wrought by Yahweh," such as the conquest of Chanaan (Jos 24,11-12), the expulsion of the marauding bands of the Madianites (Jgs 6,37; 7,2), and the liberation from Philistine domination (Jgs 15,18; 1 Sm 9,16; 19,5; 2 Sm 23,10.12).

Salvation History in the Period of the Kingdom

Like all human history, salvation history does not run in a straight, unbroken line. It has its ups and downs, and its various aspects are expressed in different ways by the various inspired writers of the Old Testament books. The history of Israel's heyday, from the conquest of Chanaan at the end of the 13th century B.C. to the fall of the kingdom of Juda at the beginning of the 6th century B.C., is not told in the Bible for its own sake. In regard to merely political or military events, important though they may now seem to us, the biblical historians are usually content to refer the reader to the now-lost chronicles of the kings of Israel and Juda. What is of primary interest to these inspired writers is Israel's religious history. The so-called deuteronomistic editors of the books of Judges, Samuel, and Kings find the reason for the vicissitudes in Israel's political life in the covenant concept of salvation history: when the Israelites are faithful to Yahweh, they prosper; when they are unfaithful to Him, they are chastised by various misfortunes.

The institution of royalty in Israel is one of the principal milestones along the road of its salvation history. Samuel, the seer and last of the charismatic "judges," was not at all sure that kingship was in keeping with God's will; it looked to him like a rejection of Yahweh as Israel's only king (1 Sm 8,7). Yet kingship was also a part of God's plan of salvation. Not that the kings themselves, except for a few, contributed much to Israel's spiritual welfare. But the great oracle which Nathan gave to David in Yahweh's name, promising him an everlasting "house," i.e., dynasty (2 Sm 7; 1 Par 22; Ps 88 [89], 20-38), was to have profound repercussions throughout the following centuries and to form the basis of Israel's Messianic expectations—the hope during the dark days of the Exile and the restoration that God would raise up the "anointed one" (for such is the meaning of the Hebrew word, *mešîḥ*, and its Greek translation, *christos*), the descendant of David who would be the great savior of Israel.

The historical books of the Old Testament outline the rugged course which Israel's salvation history actually took—the failure of the kings to keep the people faithful to Yahweh, the purifying chastisement of the Assyrian and Babylonian exile, and the postexilic restoration, which was another proof of Yahweh's ḥesed and ʾĕmet, His "loyal devotedness" and His "fidelity" to His covenant with Israel.

Salvation History in the Preexilic Prophets

Israel's prophets also had great influence on its salvation history. This was not merely due to their efforts to direct Israel's political history, as in the role which Isaia played in strengthening Juda's determination to resist the Syro-Ephraim coalition (Is 7), or in the unsuccessful endeavors of Jeremia to have Juda remain submissive to the over-lordship of Babylon. The prophets also fostered the hope of a better, Messianic future under the rule of a more worthy descendant of David than the present ruler. At first such oracles of the prophets were concerned, not with the distant future, but with a new king who would reign in the near future. Thus, the well-known oracle of Isaia about the son of the ʿalmah who would bear the symbolic name of Emmanuel ʿimmanû'ēl, "With-us-is-God," with His help)—an oracle which was later to be interpreted in a deeper Messianic sense (Mt 1,23)—referred originally to a boy at the time of the Syro-Ephraimite threat against Juda, for, before this boy would be old enough to distinguish right from wrong, Syria and Ephraim would no longer be a threat to Juda (Is 7,10-16; cf. also 8,3-10). Probably to be connected with this oracle is the same prophet's magnificent "Prince-of-Peace" oracle (Is 8,23b-9,6), which was also to be interpreted later in a broader Messianic sense (cf. Mt 4,15-16; Lk 1,32-33):

Anguish has taken wing, dispelled is darkness:
  for there is no gloom where but now there was distress.
The people who walked in darkness
  have seen a great light;
Upon those who dwelt in the land of gloom
  a light has shone.
You have brought them abundant joy
  and great rejoicing,
As they rejoice before you at the harvest,
  as men make merry when dividing spoils.
For the yoke that burdened them,
  the pole of their taskmaster
  you have smashed, as on the day of Madian.
For every boot that tramped in battle,
  every cloak rolled in blood,
  will be burned as fuel for flames.

For a child is born to us, a son is given us;
  upon his shoulder dominion rests.
They name him Wonder-Counselor, God-Hero,
  Father-Forever, Prince of Peace.
His dominion is vast
  and forever peaceful,
From David's throne, and over his kingdom,
  which he confirms and sustains
By judgment and justice,
  both now and forever.
The zeal of Yahweh Sabaoth will do this!

The Messianic "Sprout" Theme

Shortly before the Babylonian conquest of Jerusalem, when Jeremia foresaw that, with the death of Juda's last king, Sedecia, the Davidic dynasty would be brought to an end, this prophet foretold that God would raise up a new king in the house of David who would bring Juda salvation and peace.

> Behold, the days are coming, says Yahweh,
>   when I will raise up a righteous shoot to David;
> As king he shall reign and govern wisely,
>   he shall do what is just and right in the land.
> In his days Juda shall be saved,
>   Israel shall dwell in security.
> This is the name they give him:
>   "Yahweh-is-our-Justice."

In this oracle (Jer 23,5-6) the prohpet makes a strong contrast between the unjust, wicked king, Sedecia, and the new "righteous shoot of David," whose symbolic name, *Yahweh ṣidqēnû*, "Yahweh is our justice," contains a clear allusion to Sedecia's name, *Ṣidqî-Yāh*, "My justice is Yahweh." The postexilic author of Jer 33,14-26, who incorporated this oracle (33,15-16) in his prose addition to the book of Jeremia, is even more emphatic in his assertion that "never shall David lack a successor on the throne of the house of Israel" (33,17).

The same "sprout" theme occurs in an oracle attributed to Isaia (Is 11,1-5), though apparently written long after his time, when "the tree of Jesse," the dynasty founded by Jesse's son, David, had been cut down, so that only its stump remained in the exiled descendants of Jechonia.

> A shoot shall sprout from the stump of Jesse,
>   and from his roots a bud shall blossom.
> The spirit of Yahweh shall rest upon him:
>   a spirit of wisdom and of understanding,
> A spirit of counsel and of strength,
>   a spirit of knowledge and of awe of Yahweh.

A little further on in this chapter the same inspired writer refers to this Messianic sprout as "the root of Jesse," in a passage which St. Paul (Rom 15,12) interprets as foretelling the entrance of the Gentiles into the Church, the kingdom of the Messiah, "The root of Jesse, set up as a signal for the nations, the Gentiles shall seek out, for his dwelling shall be glorious" (Is 11,10). The figure of the *semaḥ* ("sprout, shoot, branch") probably goes back to Is 4,2 (an oracle of uncertain date, which also contains the theme of the "remnant"—see below), where, however, the *semaḥ Yahweh* has rather the meaning of "what Yahweh produces," as implied by the context: "The branch of Yahweh will be luster and glory, and the fruit of the earth will be honor and splendor for the survivors of Israel."

About the year 520 B.C., when the Jews were hoping that Jechonia's grandson, Zorobabel, would be able to restore the Davidic dynasty (cf. Ag 2,20-23), the prophet Zacharia, speaking in Yahweh's name, calls this prince "my servant, the Shoot" (Za 3,8; cf. 6,9-12). Yet it was not God's will that Zorobabel should "raise up the fallen hut of David" (Am 9,11). The true messianic salvation was not to come till several centuries later.

As hopes dimmed for an immediate restoration of the Davidic dynasty, Israel's Messianic expectations took on an apocalyptic coloring, and the seers looked forward to a *David redivivus*. "On that day, says Yahweh Sabaoth, 'I will break his yoke from off your necks and snap your bands.' Strangers shall no longer enslave them; instead, they shall serve Yahweh, their God, and David, their king, whom I will raise up for them" (Jer 3,8-9). "I will save my sheep so that they may no longer be despoiled, and I will judge between one sheep and another. I will appoint one shepherd over them to pasture them, my servant David; he shall pasture them and be their shepherd. I, Yahweh, will be their God, and my servant David shall be prince among them" (Ez 34,22-24). "Then the people of Israel shall turn back and seek Yahweh, their God, and David, their king" (Os 3,5).

Eschatological Typology: The New Exodus

The exilic and postexilic periods, however, not only witnessed a longing for the restoration of the Davidic kingdom; it looked to the new age as a renewal of the Mosaic period, when God's great deeds of salvation had been so clearly manifseted. The prophet Osee had already seen that the only hope of the people's moral regeneration lay in a return to the spirit of Israel's years in the desert under Moses' guidance. Speaking of Yahweh's wayward spouse, Israel, he says: "I will allure her, I will lead her into the desert and speak to her heart. From there I will give her the vineyards she had, and the valley of Achor as a door of hope. She shall respond there as in the days of her

youth, when she came up from the land of Egypt"
(Os 2,16-17).

Similarly, when Jeremia foretells the return of the people of the Northern Kingdom of Israel from their Assyrian
captivity, he alludes to the early wanderings of the Israelites in the desert before they came to their "rest" in the
Promised Land: "Thus says Yahweh: The people that
escaped the sword have found favor in the desert. As
Israel comes forward to be given his rest, Yahweh appears
to him from afar. With age-old love I have loved you; so
I have kept my mercy toward you" (Jer 31, 2-3).

For Ezechiel, the exiles from Juda who said in Babylonia, "We will be like the nations, like the peoples of
foreign lands, serving wood and stone," are similar to the
rebellious Israelites in the desert at the time of Moses:
"What you are thinking of shall never happen . . . As I
live, says Lord Yahweh, with a mighty hand and outstretched arm, with poured-out wrath, I swear I will be
king over you! . . . I will lead you to the desert of the
peoples, where I will enter into judgment with you face
to face. Just as I entered into judgment with your fathers
in the desert of the land of Egypt, so will I enter into
judgment with you, says Lord Yahweh" (Ez 20,32-36).

A more consoling note is struck by the exilic author of
Is 11, who regards the return of the exiles to Palestine as
foreshadowed in Israel's exodus and first entrance into the
Promised Land: "There shall be a highway for the remnant of his people that is left from Assyria, as there was
for Israel when he came up from the land of Egypt"
(Is 11,16). So also, when the great exilic author of the
magnificent section of Is 40-55, who, since we do not
know his name, is now commonly called "Deutero-Isaia,"

exhorts the exiles to leave Babylonia and return to Palestine, he alludes to the precipitate flight of the Israelites
from Egypt (Ex 12,11), with Yahweh's shielding column
of cloud and fire in front and in back of them (Ex 13,21-
22; 14,19-20).

> Depart, depart, come forth from there,
>   touch nothing unclean!
> Out from there! Purify yourselves,
>   you who carry the vessels of Yahweh.
> Yet not in fearful haste will you come out,
>   nor leave in headlong flight,
> For Yahweh comes before you,
>   and your rear guard is the God of Israel (Is 52,11–12).

Eschatological Typology: The New Covenant

Just as the climax of the Mosaic age was the covenant
which Yahweh made with Israel at Mount Sinai, so also,
in the Messianic age, "when Yahweh brings back the cap-
tives of Sion" (Ps 125; 126,1), He will renew His covenant with them, or rather, He will make with them a
"new covenant" (cf. Lk 22,20; 1 Cor 11,25) that will be
far superior to the old Sinaitic covenant.

Jeremia is the chief propounder of this "new covenant."
For him, this new pact between Yahweh and Israel is on
a grander scale than the old one, for: (1) it will not be
broken, as Israel had broken the Mosaic pact, but it will
last forever; (2) it will be written, not on tablets of stone,
but on the human heart (cf. Rom 2,15; 2 Cor 3,3); and
(3) it will be taught, not by human wisdom, but by God's
spirit working directly on the human spirit. "The days

are coming, say Yahweh, when I will make a new covenant with the house of Israel and the house of Juda. It
will not be like the covenant I made with their fathers
the day I took them by the hand to lead them forth from
the land of Egypt; for they broke my covenant, and I
had to show myself their master, says Yahweh. For this
is the covenant which I will make with the house of
Israel after those days, says Yahweh. I will place my law
within them and write it upon their hearts. I will be their
God, and they shall be my people. No longer will they
have need to teach their friends and kinsmen how to know
Yahweh. All, from least to greatest, shall know me, says
Yahweh, for I will forgive their evildoing and remember
their sin no more" (Jer 31,31-34). "Behold, I will gather
them together from all the lands to which in anger, wrath,
and great rage I banish them; I will bring them back to
this place and settle them here in safety. They shall be
my people, and I will be their God . . . I will make with
them an eternal covenant, never to cease doing good to
them; into their hearts I will put the fear of me, that they
may never depart from me" (Jer 32,36-40).

But Ezechiel also is acquainted with this theme of the
"new covenant." Likening the Sinaitic covenant to a marriage bond between Yahweh and Israel, this prophet, after
his long, scathing rebuke to Israel for proving an adulterous
wife (Ez 16,1-58), presents Yahweh as being willing to
forgive her infidelity and renew His marriage covenant
with her. "For thus speaks Lord Yahweh: I will deal with
you according to what you have done, you who despised
your oath, breaking your covenant. Yet I will remember
the covenant I made with you when you were a girl, and

I will set up an everlasting covenant with you . . . even though I am not bound by my covenant with you. For I will re-establish my covenant with you, that you may know that I am Yahweh, that you may remember and be covered with confusion, and that you may be utterly silenced for shame when I pardon you for all you have done, says Lord Yahweh (Ez 16, 59-63). This "new covenant" is intimately connected with the forgiveness of the people's sins, and it is clearly Messianic, for it is to be realized in the eschatological age of the *David redivivus*: "No longer shall they defile themselves with their idols, their abominations, and all their transgressions. I will deliver them from all their sins of apostasy, and cleanse them so that they may be my people and I may be their God. My servant David shall be prince over them, and there shall be one shepherd for them all . . . They shall live on the land which I gave to my servant Jacob . . . with my servant David their prince forever. I will make with them a covenant of peace; it shall be an everlasting covenant with them, and I will multiply them, and put my sanctuary among them forever" (Ez 37,23-26).

Eschatological Typology: Paradise Restored

For the prophets, the new Messianic age of salvation is to be such a marvelous restoration of pristine bliss that they depict it as a new paradise on earth, an era of happiness and prosperity, of idyllic peace, not only among men, but even among the wild animals. "I will make a covenant for them on that day, with the beasts of the field, with the birds of the air, and with the things that crawl on the ground. Bow and sword and war I will destroy from the land, and I will let them take their rest in security" (Os 2,20). "Yes, days are coming, says Yahweh, when the plowman shall overtake the reaper, and the vintager, him who sows the seed. The juice of grapes shall drip down the mountains, and all the hills shall run with it" (Am 9,13). "And then, on that day, the mountains shall drip new wine, and the hills shall flow with milk; and the channels of Juda shall flow with water: a fountain shall issue from the house of Yahweh, to water the Valley of Sattim" (Jl 4,18; cf. Ez 47,1-12). "I will make a covenant of peace with them, and rid the country of ravenous beasts, that they may dwell securely in the desert and sleep in the forests" (Ez 34,25).

> Then the wolf shall be a guest of the lamb,
>   and the leopard shall lie down with the kid;
> The calf and the young lion shall browse together,
>   with a little child to guide them.
> The cow and the bear shall be neighbors,
>   together their young shall rest;
>   the lion shall eat hay like the ox.
> The baby shall play by the cobra's den,
>   and the child lay his hand on the adder's lair.
> There shall be no harm or ruin on all my holy mountain;
>   for the earth shall be filled with knowledge of Yahweh,
>   as water covers the sea (Is 11,6-9).

The Remnant of Israel

An important theme in Israel's salvation history is that of the "remnant." This *šeʾar yiśrāʾēl* or *šeʾērît yiśrāʾel*, "rem-

nant of Israel," refers to a certain select group in Israel
that is saved by God's merciful providence from the general chastisement in which the others perish. The general
idea of God choosing for Himself a "remnant" for salvation is a very old one. Thus, in Gn 45,7 Joseph tells his
brothers, "God sent me before you to preserve a remnant
for you in the land and to rescue you in a striking way."
In fact, this concept is present even in the ancient story
of the Deluge: "Only Noe and those with him in the
ark were left" (Gn 7,23). In these passages the "remnant"
is, in a sense, the whole Chosen People. But in 3 Kgs
19,17-18 the remnant is only a part of the whole people:
in the massacre inflicted by Jehu, God leaves for Himself
seven thousand men who did not worship Baal.

This technical sense of the term is especially common
in the prophets. Thus, Amos says of the Northern Kingdom of Israel, "The eyes of Lord Yahweh are on this
sinful kingdom: I will destroy it from off the face of the
earth. But I will not destroy the House of Jacob completely" (Am 9,8). That a certain select group in Israel
is preserved by Yahweh for Himself is expressly stated
by Jeremia and Sophonia: "I will forgive the remnant I
preserve" (Jer 50,20); "I will leave as a remnant in your
midst a people humble and lowly, who shall take refuge
in the name of Yahweh: the remnant of Israel" (So 3,12).
In several passages the "remnant" is synonymous with
Yahweh's people who are in exile: "Yahweh shall again
take it in hand to reclaim the remnant of his people that
is left from Assyria and Egypt" etc. (Is 11,11; cf. also
v. 16); "Hear me, O house of Jacob, all who remain of
the house of Israel" (Is 46,3); "I myself will gather the

remnant of my flock from all the lands to which I have driven them and bring them back to their meadow" (Jer 23,3); "I will assemble all the remant of Israel" (Mi 2,12). Later, the Jews who returned to Palestine from their exile in Babylonia constitute "the remnant" (Za 8,6.11–12); but even of this remnant a special group is chosen by God for further purification:

> In all the land, says Yahweh,
>> two thirds of them shall be cut off and perish,
>> and one third shall be left.
> I will bring the one third through fire,
>> and I will refine them as silver is refined,
>> and I will test them as gold is tested.
> They shall call upon my name,
>> and I will hear them.
> I will say, "They are my people,"
>> and they shall say, "Yahweh is my God" (Za 13,8–9)

It is to be noted, however, that, while on the one hand "the remnant" forms an ever-decreasing circle—first all mankind, then only Israel, and finally an ever-smaller group in Israel, on the other hand the circle of "the remnant" will eventually become broader and broader—first a reunited Israel, and then a new Israel that embraces even the Gentiles. After Juda is reduced to a miserable condition, it will strike new roots and experience a new flowering of power and prosperity.

> The remaining survivors of the house of Juda
>> shall again strike root below
>> and bear fruit above.
> For out of Jerusalem shall come a remnant
>> and from Mount Sion, survivors.
>> The zeal of Yahweh Sabaoth shall do this. (Is 37–31–32)

The poor and lowly people of "the remnant" who return to God with a sincere heart (Is 10,20–21) and
receive from Him the pardon of their sins (Jer 50,20) shall
become a mighty nation and, with Yahweh as its king,
form a realm that embraces even the pagans.

> On that day, says Yahweh,
>   I will gather the lame,
> And I will assemble the outcasts
>   and those whom I have afflicted.
> I will make of the lame a remnant,
>   and of those driven far off a strong nation;
> And Yahweh shall be king over them on Mount Sion,
>   from now and forever. (Mi 4,6–7)

> The remnant of Jacob shall be
>   in the midst of many peoples,
> Like dew coming from Yahweh,
>   like raindrops on the grass,
> Which wait for no man,
>   nor tarry for the sons of men.
> And the remnant of Jacob shall be among the nations,
>   in the midst of many peoples,
> Like a lion among beasts of the forest,
>   like a young lion among flocks of sheep. (Mi 5,6–7)

> On that day Yahweh Sabaoth
>   will be a glorious crown
> And a brilliant diadem
>   to the remnant of his people. (Is 28,5)

> I will destroy the pride of the Philistine
>   and take from his mouth his bloody meat. . . .
> He also shall become a remnant for our God,
>   and he shall be like a family in Juda. (Za 9,6–7)

Salvation History in Deutero-Isaia

At the end of the Babylonian exile the anonymous prophet known as Deutero-Isaia (Is 40–55) brings the "salvation" theme as such to its greatest development, using "salvation" terminology no less than twenty-one times. For him, Yahweh is Israel's only savior: "It is I, I Yahweh; there is no savior but me. It is I who foretold, I who saved; I made it known, not any strange god among you" (Is 43,11–12; cf. also 45,15.21). The Lord's rescue of His people from their exile in Babylonia is like a new creation.

> I am Yahweh, there is no other;
>> I form the light and create the darkness,
> I make well-being and create woe;
>> I, Yahweh, do all these things.
> Let justice descend, O heavens, like dew from above,
>> like gentle rain let the skies drop it down.
> Let the earth open and salvation bud forth;
>> let justice also spring up!
>> I, Yahweh, have created this. (Is 45,6b–8)

Salvation and Justice in Deutero-Isaia

Typical of Deutero-Isaia is the combination of the salvation wrought by God with His "justice" (*ṣedeq* and *ṣedāqâ*). He has Yahweh say, "There is no just (*ṣaddîq*) and saving God but me" (Is 45,21). The Lord, he argues, will not fail to save Israel because He is "just," that is, upright and honest, and therefore faithful to His covenant promises. This is the so-called "salvific justice" of God which is of prime importance in the Pauline doctrine of man's "justification": "The justice of God has been made manifest . . . , the justice of God through faith in Jesus Christ upon all who believe. . . . They are justified freely by his grace . . . , to manifest that he himself is just and makes just him who has faith in Jesus" (Rom 3,21–26).

Thus, in assuring Israel that its salvation (i.e., return from exile) is at hand, Deutero-Isaia has the Lord say,

> I am bringing on my justice, it is not far off,
>   my salvation shall not tarry;
> I will put salvation within Sion
>   and give to Israel my glory. (Is 46,13)

In fact, not only Israel, but all the world shall soon experience the salvation that Yahweh is to bring:

> I will make my justice come speedily,
>   my salvation shall come forth;
> In me shall the coastlands hope,
>   and my arm they shall await. (Is 51,5; cf. also 52,10)

Salvation and Redemption in Deutero-Isaia

Lack of space prevents a full presentation here of the "redemption" theme which forms a special aspect of the "salvation" theme throughout the Old Testament. Suffice it here to say that this special concept is expressed in Hebrew by two closely related, but distinct sets of terms: those based on the verb *pādâ*, which signifies the paying of a ransom price for one's freedom, and those based on the verb *gā'al*, which designates the action of one who rescues a kinsman from some predicament.

The former verb is often used, not only of Yahweh's deed in "redeeming," i.e., freeing, the Israelites from their Egyptian bondage (Dt 9,26; 15,15; 21,8; 24,18; etc.), but also of His delivering them from their Babylonian captivity (Jer 31,11; Za 10,8). In Deutero-Isaia, however, the use of this term to express the Lord's salvific deeds is rare, though it does occur.

> Is my hand too short to ransom?
> Have I not the strength to deliver? (Is 50,2)

On the other hand, terms from the verb *gā'al*, which are also used in other parts of the Old Testament to designate Yahweh as the *gō'ēl*, "rescuing kinsman" and therefore "redeemer" of Israel ("kinsman" because of His covenant relationship with Israel), both in regard to the Exodus from Egypt (Ex 6,6; 15,13, etc.) and in regard to the return from the Babylonian exile (Jer 31,11; Mi 4,10), are particularly frequent in Deutero-Isaia. For this prophet, Yahweh is Israel's *gō'ēl* (Is 41,14; 43,14; 44,24; 47,4; 48,17; 49,7; 54,5), for He is also the creator (43,1.7.15; 44,6.21.24; 54,5), the "chooser" (44,1; 49,1) and the bridegroom (54,4) of Israel. Yahweh is Israel's "redeemer," not only because He rescues it from exile (43,14; 48,20) or from every other misfortune (41,14; 43,1-3), but also because He exalts it before the eyes of all the nations (49,7.23; cf. 60,16). Yet Israel's splendor in the world is but the reflection of its inner, spiritual renewal, which consists in Yahweh's wiping out of Israel's sins (44,22;

cf. 50,1) and of His teaching Israel to walk on the way of salvation (48,17). In this redemption Yahweh "shows forth his glory through Israel" (44,23) and expresses His undying love for Israel: "With enduring love I take pity on you, says Yahweh, your redeemer" (54,8; cf. v. 10). That this redemption is essentially spiritual is shown by the often repeated combination of the term *gōʾēl* with Yahweh's title, "the Holy One of Israel" (41,14; 43,14; 49,7; 54,5). On account of Deutero-Isaia's stress on Yahweh's salvation of Israel as a redemption, the Jews in the last pre-Christian centuries spoke of the expected Messianic salvation as *geʾullat yiśrāēl*, "the redemption of Israel," a term which is likewise used in Lk 2,38 (cf. also Lk 1,68).

The "Servant of Yahweh" Oracles in Deutero-Isaia

An extremely important element in salvation history is introduced in the four so-called *ʿebed Yahweh* ("the Servant of the Lord") oracles in Deutero-Isaia. This "Servant" is certainly a *Heilsfigur*, a figure intimately connected with salvation history. But at the same time he is also a very mysterious figure.

While he is generally presented as distinct from Israel, at least once (49,3) he is identified with Israel. Although he has certain Messianic traits, especially in his being God's agent for saving both Israel and "the nations," he is nowhere described in terms of an anointed king, and apparently he was not identified with the expected Messiah in pre-Christian Judaism. The most remarkable thing, however, about him is his function in atoning for the sins of men by his vicarious sufferings—an idea that never finds expression anywhere else in the Old Testament. Although we may not be able to determine with certainty just what Deutero-Isaia himself directly understood by the words of these oracles, there is no doubt at all about the fact that in the New Testament Jesus of Nazareth is presented as the complete fulfillment of this prophetic figure.

These four oracles, in their minimal extent (there being some doubts as to how far the first three of them should run), are as follows.

> Here is my servant whom I uphold,
>   my chosen one with whom I am pleased,
> Upon whom I have put my spirit;
>   he shall bring forth justice to the nations,
> Not crying out, not shouting,
>   not making his voice heard in the street.
> A bruised reed he shall not break,
>   and a smoldering wick he shall not quench,
> Until he establishes justice on the earth;
>   the coastlands will wait for his teaching. (Is 42,1–4)

> Hear me, O coastlands,
>   listen, O distant peoples.
> Yahweh called me from birth,
>   from my mother's womb he gave me my name.
> He made of me a sharp-edged sword
>   and concealed me in the shadow of his arm.
> He made me a polished arrow,
>   in his quiver he hid me.
> You are my servant, he said to me,
>   Israel, through whom I show my glory.

> Though I thought I had toiled in vain,
>   and for nothing, uselessly, spent my strength,

Yet my reward is with Yahweh,
  my recompense is with my God.
For now Yahweh has spoken
  who formed me as his servant from the womb,
That Jacob may be brought back to him
  and Israel gather to him;
And I am made glorious in the sight of Yahweh,
  and my God is now my strength!
It is too little, he says, for you to be my servant,
  to raise up the tribes of Jacob,
  and restore the survivors of Israel;
I will make you a light to the nations,
  that my salvation may reach
  to the ends of the earth. (Is 49,1–6)

Lord Yahweh has given me
  a well-trained tongue,
That I might know how to speak to the weary
  a word that will rouse them.
Morning after morning
  he opens my ear that I may hear;
And I have not rebelled,
  have not turned back.
I gave my back to those who beat me,
  my cheeks to those who plucked my beard;
My face I did not shield
  from buffets and spitting.

Lord Yahweh is my help,
  therefore I am not disgraced;
I have set my face like flint,
  knowing that I shall not be put to shame.
He is near who upholds my right;
  if anyone wishes to oppose me,
  let us appear together.
Who disputes my right?
  Let him confront me.

See, Lord Yahweh is my help;
   who will prove me wrong?
Lo, they will all wear out like cloth,
   the moth will eat them up. (Is 50,4–9)

See, my servant shall prosper,
   he shall be raised high and greatly exalted.
Even as many were amazed at him—
   so marred was his look beyond that of man,
   and his appearance beyond that of mortals—
So shall he startle many nations,
   because of him kings shall stand speechless;
For those who have not been told shall see,
   those who have not heard shall ponder it.

Who would believe what we have heard?
   To whom has the arm of Yahweh been revealed?
He grew up like a sapling before him,
   like a shoot from the parched earth;
There was in him no stately bearing to make us look at him,
   nor appearance that would attract us to him.
He was spurned and voided by men,
   a man of suffering, accustomed to infirmity,
One of those from whom men hide their faces,
   spurned, and we held him in no esteem.

Yet it was our infirmities that he bore,
   our sufferings that he endured,
While we thought of him as stricken,
   as one smitten by God and afflicted.
But he was pierced for our offenses,
   crushed for our sins;
Upon him was the chastisement that makes us whole,
   by his stripes we were healed.
We had all gone astray like sheep,
   each following his own way;
But Yahweh laid upon him
   the guilt of us all.

Though he was harshly treated, he submitted
    and opened not his mouth;
Like a lamb led to the slaughter
    or a sheep before the shearers,
    he was silent and opened not his mouth.
Oppressed and condemned, he was taken away,
    and who would have thought any more of his destiny?
When he was cut off from the land of the living,
    and smitten for the sin of his people,
A grave was assigned him among the wicked
    and a burial place with evildoers,
Though he had done no wrong
    nor spoken any falsehood . . .

If he gives his life as an offering for sin,
    he shall see his descendants in a long life,
    and the will of Yahweh
    shall be accomplished through him.
Because of his affliction
    he shall see the light in fullness of days;
Through his suffering, my servant shall justify many,
    and their guilt he shall bear.
Therefore I will give him his portion among the great,
    and he shall divide the spoils with the mighty,
Because he surrendered himself to death
    and was counted among the wicked;
And he shall take away the sins of many,
    and win pardon for their offenses. (Is 52,13–53,12)

Eschatological Aspects of Salvation

In the last pre-Christian centuries, when "the redemption
of Israel" seemed to delay ever more and more in coming,
Israel's expectation of salvation took on many eschatologi-

cal features, especially under the influence of the apocalyptic writers. Biblical eschatology, i.e., what would happen *beʾaḥărît hayyāmîm* (Gn 49,1; Nm 24,14; Dt 4,30; 31,29; Is 2,2; Jer 23,20, etc.), literally, "at the end of days," i.e., at the end of time, is too complicated a matter to be treated here with any adequacy. It will be sufficient for the present purpose to say merely a few words on two eschatological concepts: the Day of the Lord, and the establishment of the Kingdom of God.

The Day of the Lord

The concept of *yôm Yahweh*, or often simply *hayyôm*, "*the* Day," by which is meant the expected great intervention of Yahweh in the affairs of men, goes back to pre-exilic times in Israel. As early as the middle of the 8th century B.C. the prophet Amos has to combat the popular notion that, despite the sins of Israel, the Day of Yahweh would surely bring nothing but victory, peace and prosperity for all the Chosen People: "Woe to those who yearn for the Day of Yahweh! . . . Will not the Day of Yahweh be darkness and not light?" (Am 5,18-20). So also, most of the prophets stress the element of chastisement, rather than that of salvation, when they announce the coming Day of Yahweh. For them this day is primarily one of wrath against the enemies of the Lord; cf., e.g., Is 2,6-22; So 1,2-18 (especially v. 15: *dies irae, dies illa!*); Ez 7; Jl 2,1-17.

But at the same time, if the Day of Yahweh is one of punishment for the wicked, it is also regarded as one of salvation for the just. The latter aspect is stressed particularly by the postexilic prophets, when "the remnant of Israel" stood in need of consolation and encouragement. Thus Joel, who can predict dire woe for the wicked, can also depict the future happiness of the just on the Day of Yahweh.

> The sun will be turned to darkness,
>   and the moon to blood,
> At the coming of the Day of Yahweh,
>   the great and terrible day.
> Then everyone shall be rescued
>   who calls on the name of Yahweh;
> For on Mount Sion there shall be a remnant,
>   as Yahweh has said,
> And in Jerusalem survivors
>   whom Yahweh shall call.
>
> Yes, in those days and at that time,
>   when I would restore the fortunes
>   of Juda and Jerusalem,
> I will assemble all the nations
>   and bring them down to the Valley of Josaphat,
> And I will enter into judgment with them there
>   on behalf of my people
>   and my inheritance, Israel. (Jl 3,4–4,2)

So also in Za 14, where the coming Day of Yahweh is described as "a day of battle" on which the Lord shall overwhelm the enemies of Israel, this eschatological day is depicted as one of paradisiacal happiness: "On that day there shall no longer be cold or frost. There shall be one continuous day, know to Yahweh, not day and night, for in the evening time there shall be light. On that day, living waters shall flow from Jerusalem, half to the eastern sea, and half to the western sea, and it shall be so in summer and in winter" (Za 14,6-8). Likewise, in Mal 3, after Yahweh sends His messenger to prepare the way before Him, He Himself will come to His temple and purify the sons of Levi (vv. 1-3) in a fire that will burn up the wicked (v. 19).

The Establishment of the Kingdom of God

The title of "King" was apparently not applied to Yahweh before the introduction of human kingship in Israel. In preexilic times the kingship of Yahweh had no special soteriological connotation; the term, "King," was used of Him to suggest His triumphant majesty (Nm 23,21) or the grandeur in which He should be worshiped (Is 6,5; Ps 23 [24], 7-10). Yahweh's kingship in the so-called "Enthronement Psalms" (Ps 46 [47]; 92 [93]; 95-98 [96-99]), themselves of uncertain date, admits of various interpretations, though it is quite possible to understand these Psalms as referring to the eschatological establishment of His kingship.

In Deutero-Isaia, however, the kingship of Yahweh has definitely soteriological significance. Yahweh, "the King of Jacob" (Is 41,21), is not only "the Creator of Israel" (43,15), but also its redeemer: "Thus says Yahweh, Israel's King and redeemer, Yahweh Sabaoth . . ." (44,6). Yahweh's coming reign is to be a source of peace, happiness and salvation for His people.

> How beautiful upon the mountains
>   are the feet of him who brings glad tidings,

Announcing peace, bearing good news,
    announcing salvation, and saying to Sion,
    "Your God is King!" (Is 52,7)

There are also several postexilic oracles that depict the
exiles of Israel as returning in a glorious restoration to their
own land under the leadership of Yahweh their King.

Indeed Yahweh will be there with us, majestic;
    yes, Yahweh our judge, Yahweh our lawgiver,
    Yahweh our king, he it is who will save us. (Is 33,20)

With a leader to break the path
    they shall burst open the gate and go out through it;
Their king shall go through before them,
    and Yahweh at their head. (Mi 2,13)

I will make of the lame a remnant,
    and of those driven far off a strong nation;
And Yahweh shall be king over them on Mount Sion,
    from now on forever. (Mi 4,7)

Yahweh has removed the judgment against you,
    he has turned away your enemies;
The King of Israel, Yahweh, is in your midst,
    you have no further misfortune to fear. (So 3,15)

And saviors shall ascend Mount Sion
    to rule the mount of Esau,
    and the kingship shall be Yahweh's. (Abd 21)

For the apocalyptic writers, the establishment of Yahweh's reign as king will be brought about by such a
tremendous intervention on His part that the very foundation of the earth will be shaken; thus, for instance, in the
so-called "Apocalypse of Isaia" (Is 24–27):

The windows on high will be opened,
    and the foundations of the earth will shake.
The earth will burst asunder,
    the earth will be shaken apart,
    the earth will be convulsed.
The earth will reel like a drunkard,
    and it will sway like a hut;
Its rebellion will weigh it down,
    until it falls, never to rise again.

On that day Yahweh will punish
    the host of the heavens in the heavens,
    and the kings of the earth on the earth.
They will be gathered together
    like prisoners into a pit;
They will be shut up in a dungeon,
    and after many days they will be punished.
Then the moon will blush
    and the sun grow pale,
For Yahweh Sabaoth will reign
    on Mount Sion and in Jerusalem,
    glorious in the sight of his elders. (Is 24,18–23)

Similar ideas of universal upheaval are expressed in Za 14, where, finally, "all who are left of all the nations that came against Jerusalem shall come up year after year to worship the King, Yahweh Sabaoth. . . . If any of the families of the earth does not come up to Jerusalem to worship the King, Yahweh Sabaoth, no rain shall fall upon them" (Za 14,16–17).

In the apocalyptic visions of the Book of Daniel, which, at least in their present form, date from about the year 165 B.C., the four earthy kingdoms—the Assyro-Babylonian, the Median, the Persian, and the Greek kingdoms, which oppressed the people of God—are supplanted by the king-

dom of God's people, over which God reigns supreme,
and which is to last forever. "In the lifetime of those kings
the God of heaven will set up a kingdom that shall never
be destroyed or delivered to another people; rather, it shall
break in pieces all these kingdoms and put an end to them,
and it shall stand forever" (Dn 2,44).

> Then the kingship and dominion and majesty
> of all the kingdoms under the heavens
> shall be given to the holy people of the Most High,
> Whose kingdom shall be everlasting:
> all dominions shall serve and obey him.
> (Dn 7,27; cf. also 6,27)

The seer of this apocalyptic book beheld four monstrous
beasts that emerged from "the great sea," typifying the
four earthly kingdoms that were hostile to God. Then as
he watched,

> Thrones were set up
> and the Ancient One took his throne.
> His clothing was snow bright,
> and the hair on his head as white as wool;
> His throne was flames of fire,
> with wheels of burning fire.
> A surging stream of fire
> flowed out from where he sat;
> Thousands upon thousands were ministering to him,
> and myriads upon myriads attended him. (Dn 7,9-10)

The seer then saw

> One like a son of man coming,
> on the clouds of heaven;
> When he reached the Ancient One
> and was presented before him,
> He received dominion, glory, and kingship;

nations and peoples of every language serve him.
His dominion is an everlasting dominion
    that shall not be taken away,
    his kingship shall not be destroyed. (Dn 7,13–14)

In this vision the being that had human form (for this is the meaning of the expression, "one like a son of man") appears on the clouds of the sky to point the contrast with the four monstrous beings that emerge from the great sea of primeval chaos. Therefore, in the context it can only designate the kingdom of God's people, as is expressly stated in the angel's interpretation of the vision: "These four great beasts stand for four kingdoms which shall arise on the earth. But the holy ones of the Most High shall receive the kingship, to possess it forever" (Dn 7,17–18). Yet the term, "Son of Man," which Jesus Christ used so often in speaking of Himself, is certainly derived from this passage (cf. Mk 14,62). Therefore, this mysterious expression, which Jesus used both to conceal and to reveal His Messiahship, is thus seen to include both the Kingdom of God and its Messianic King.

New Testament Fulfillment

Jesus of Nazareth began His ministry by "preaching the gospel of the kingdom of God and saying, 'The time is fulfilled, and the kingdom of God is at hand. Repent and believe in the gospel'" (Mk 1,14–15). The whole New Testament is the fulfillment of all the Old Testament's promises and expectations of salvation. It is the climax of "salvation history." Every New Testament writer bears witness with Simeon: "My eyes have seen your salvation, which you have prepared for all the peoples, a light of revelation to the nations, and glory for your people, Israel" (Lk 2,3-32).

But it would go beyond the scope of the present paper to show the development of salvation history in the New Testament—a topic that has its own difficulties, as for instance, how the Kingdom of God, which has already come, but for the coming of which we are taught to pray (Mt 6,10), became the Church, or how an "anticipated eschatalogy" grew, in view of the fact that, while, in one sense, Christians already live in the Day of the Lord, this day still lies in the indetermined future, just as, in one sense, they are already saved (2,5.8), while, in another sense, their salvation still lies in the future (Rom 5,10; 13,11; 1 Thes 5,9; Heb 1,14, etc.). Suffice it here to conclude with the words of the angel to St. Joseph, "You shall call his name Jesus, for he shall save his people from their sins" (Mt 1,21), and with the words of St. Peter, "There is no other name under heaven given to men by which we must be saved" (Acts 4,12).

Existence and Redemption

▶▶

FRANCIS X. MURPHY, C.SS.R., Ph.D.

I

In the historic discourse with which he inaugurated Vatican Council II, Pope John set as one of its principal aims "a step forward toward a doctrinal penetration and a formation of consciences in faithful and perfect conformity to authentic doctrine, which, however, should be studied and expounded through the methods of research and through the literary forms of modern thought." That this objective was not far from the early Church's traditional mode of operation is indicated by the manner in which the early Christians faced the problems with which their faith was confronted in the announcement and development of the primitive theology. Thanks to a number of recent studies, this activity can be seen in clearer perspective with regard, for example, to the doctrine of the Redemption whose relevance to the cultural environment of the first centuries cannot be overemphasized, and which should prove a wholesome reflection for those concerned with the renewal of the Church's apostolic mission in a world today worried not only about survival but about the very implication of existence.

St. Paul gives evidence of having quickly realized that the Christian Gospel was not received in the Jewish or Hellenistic world with the sympathy or joy that one would expect of those hearing the "good news" of their deliverance from interior worries or from the powers of evil which it represented. In his Letter to the Corinthians, for example, he admits: "The doctrine of the Cross is foolishness to those who are perishing . . . (since) the world did not come to know God by (secular) wisdom. . . . The Jews ask for a sign and the Greeks for wisdom; but we preach Christ crucified, to the Jews a stumbling block, and to the Gentiles foolishness, but to those who are called, both Jew and Greek, the power of God and the wisdom of God" (I Cor 1,18–25).

What Paul had in mind by *wisdom* is the way of salvation, the final realization of God's plan in creation, and this is in keeping with the old rabbinic tradition of his cultural milieu that identified the "way of wisdom" or *hokmah* with the right conduct of life. When writing to the Thessalonians, adapting his thought to the needs of his age, Paul contrasts the two ways of life currently being led among them, and speaks of the night as "the time for revelry and sleep" characteristic of the pagan conduct; while the life of the Christians as "children of light and of the day" has been given a new status, for they are called to live in a new order in which a godly motivated approach to life and self-discipline are required (1 Thes 5,6–8).

In the attempt to restate the message of Christ so as to make its essential truth and relevance clear to their contemporaries, neither Paul nor his fellow apostles had any intention of betraying the fundamental facts of that revelation, for again, as he testifies, he was fully conscious of the danger of preaching "another Gospel and another Jesus" (2 Cor 11,4). What he did was to announce "to the Jews first, then to the Gentiles," the important news of the life and death of Jesus Christ in brief form, demonstrating that in Christ's conflict, sufferings, death and resurrection, the divinely guided destiny of Israel had reached its climax. God himself had now personally entered into the history of mankind to inaugurate His Kingdom on earth, and as the Savior Himself had said, He had come to "cast fire on the earth" and desired that through His disciples the whole world should be enlightened and enkindled with a new life.

It seems obvious that from the beginning of the apostles' preaching attention was turned to the conditions of the times and account was taken of the desire for deliverance widely spread throughout the Judaic and Hellenic atmosphere. Hence an assertion of redemption in Christ quickly became an essential feature of the *lex orandi*, or law of prayer, best preserved perhaps in Paul's assurance to the Corinthians that "according to the Gospel I preached to you . . . first of all, and which I also received, Christ died for our sins according to the Scriptures" (1 Cor 15,1.3).

It is surprising, however, that the development of this doctrine of salvation whereby St. Paul exhorts the Christians of Rome to utilize their faith to achieve "peace with God through our Lord Jesus Christ" and to "exult in the hope of glory of the Son of God" is not discernible in the immediately post-apostolic documents that reflect the mind of the Church at the end of the first and the early part of the second century. For in his letters to both the

Romans and the Philippians, Paul exhorted the Christians "to exult in tribulations, knowing that tribulation works out endurance, and endurance tried virtue, and tried virtue hope," and all this in "the charity of God which is poured out in our hearts by the Holy Spirit." Paul asks his readers: "For why did Christ die at a set time for the wicked, when as yet we were weak?," only to answer the question by assuring them: "Now that we are justified by His blood, we shall be saved through Him from the wrath. For if when we were enemies we were reconciled to God by the death of His Son, much more having been reconciled shall we be saved by His life." And Paul goes on to discuss the question of the relation between grace and sin, between the old Law and Christian freedom (Rom 6-8).

The oldest post-biblical document, the *Didache*, while laying out guidelines for Christian conduct, is still very much of a Jewish product, and does not directly refer to the Redemption, but speaks only of "knowledge, life, faith and immortality," brought about through Christ "in connection with the Eucharist" (9,3; 10,2), and the *Letter of the Pseudo-Barnabas*, which also betrays Hebraic antecedents, merely hints at salvation for the individual by stating cryptically: "Blessed are those who fix their hope on the Cross and have descended into the water" meaning, of course, baptism, since it describes at some length the Savior's intimation throughout the Old Testament of the efficacy of water and the Cross (Chap. 11). The *Letter of Clement* written from Rome to the community at Corinth about A.D. 100 advises obedience to God's commands "because of Christ's Passion" (1,3) and insists on the necessity of penance "in consideration of Christ's having shed his blood for us" (8,1-5). These documents are the products of a fundamentally Judaic atmosphere in which, particularly in the *Letter of Clement,* there are also obvious infiltrations of a Stoic doctrine concerning the created order in the universe and man's moral obligations.

It is only with Ignatius of Antioch (*c.* 116 A.D.) that a first full step is discernible in the adaptation of the Christian Gospel to the requirements of the strictly Hellenic or secular viewpoint of the age. In contrast to St. Paul who is struggling with the demands of the old Law and of righteousness as they continue to affect the Jewish conscience even after the acceptance of Christ, Ignatius reflects the preoccupations of the Greek mind faced with the experience of daily destruction and of death, and its longing for an imperishable life. Thus, in proclaiming the redemption in Christ to his contemporaries, Ignatius speaks of the Eucharist as "the medicine of immortality, the antidote to death" (*Epistle to the Trallians,* 5), and describes the necessity under which men labor of being rescued from the demons, the demons being credited by both Jewish and pagan beliefs with being a source of destruction and sin for mankind. Besides, Ignatius calls for a complete transformation of mentality in the believer, a transformation to be brought about by regeneration in Christ and God through baptism. The Christian is one who "imitates Christ in His Passion." This is to be the motivation of his daily life. Death in and with Christ will then be a welcome consummation of the union with God that he strives for in the practice of virtue, and particularly of charity (*agape*) which is the gift of oneself in and to the community; and the community is in turn the body of Christ and the Church" (Eph 10,1–3; 14,1–2; Smyr 6,2–7).

However, it is with the body of writings produced by
the Apologists during the second century—Justin, Aristides,
Tatian, etc.—that we meet the first clear indication of a
crossing of the Christian Gospel with the religious movements affecting their age. We see the early Christian missionary in open competition with rival types of propaganda
—as St. Paul would have said, with that of the Jews first,
then that of the Gentiles. For while little effort was made
in Palestine by the Rabbis to convert the strangers with
whom they came into contact—unwelcome Roman ad-
ministrators and soldiers, for the most part, a few mer-
chants and the other Semitic peoples from outside
Palestine—the situation was considerably different among
the colonies of Jews settled in all the great cities of the
Roman Empire. Here a sustained effort was made to interest their neighbors in Jewish beliefs, and a technique
and literature were developed for the Jewish proselytizers
exemplified in the *Against Apion* of the first-century Jewish historian Josephus, and more particularly in the Alex-
andrian Jewish philosopher Philo's *Life of Moses*, his
Explanation of the Laws, and his *Apology for the Jews*,
together with his vast output of allegorical and typologi-
cal literature that demonstrate his attempt to bridge the
Jewish and Hellenic worlds. Philo achieved a considerable
success, and his effort was to have a lasting effect on the
Fathers of the Church, from Clement of Alexandria and
Tertullian in the second century to Ambrose, Augustine
and John Chrysostom in the fourth. But more directly the
early Apologists had to cross lines with the Neo-Platonic,
Stoic and Pythagorean philosophies and with the Gnostic
and esoteric mystical elements in the mystery religions that

were then striving to capture the interest of their contemporaries by their doctrines of salvation for the initiate.

In Justin Martyr the Church comes to grips simultaneously with the pagan and the Judaic milieux as he attempts to demonstrate that, by God's design, the coming of Christ and the work of the Redemption have been so ordered as to complete two converging lines of human development. This design he calls the *economy of salvation*, an expression not unknown to St. Paul, but which receives its proper utilization in Justin and will serve as the category under which Greek theology will be developed when discussing God's dealings with man outside the Trinity. In describing Christ as "the Son of God who existed before the morning star and the moon, who consented to become flesh so that, by this economy, the serpent who from the beginning had acted evilly, and the angels who imitated him, should be destroyed" (*Dialogue with Trypho the Jew*, 45,4), Justin insists that this term covers all the mysteries of Christ's being and life in the world (*Dial* 87,5) and particularly that of the Virgin birth (70,1), and the Passion (30,3). What Justin emphasizes is that Christ joins Himself to fallen mankind according to the desire of His Father, but by His own will. He connects the whole history of man as recorded particularly in the Old Testament as at once a prophecy and a prefiguration of Christ, wherein "the Patriarchs realized the economy of the great mysteries" of faith (134,2), and the "marriage of the Patriarchs is a figure of the union of Christ and His Church" (141.4).

This economy is thus the history of the relationship between the Word of God and the world carried out in accord with the Father's will from before the beginning of time; and it is Christ as the Word of God who was present in the various theophanies of the Old Testament, wherein God appeared to Abraham in the form of an angel, to Moses in the form of fire and an incorporeal figure, and in diverse manners to the other prophets (*Apol* 63,16; *Dial* 13,4-5).

Justin's ideas are shared by Theophilus of Antioch, for whom Christ's mission in the world is to destroy the tyranny of Satan and thus liberate humanity from sinfulness by the power of His Passion: "A secret power of God is in Christ crucified who makes the demons rage, particularly because of the power of the Cross which was prefigured in Isaia (9,5)." This work is continued in the Church: "Our Jesus has sent the word of appeal and of penitence to all the nations, there where the demons dominate. And His word overcoming them has convinced a great number to abandon the demons whom they served, since the demons are the gods of Satan." For Justin, again, this efficacity of Christ works through the sacraments, particularly through the Eucharist, and it is offered "in souvenir of the suffering which He endured to purify humanity. Thus we teach that the nourishment consecrated by the word of prayer comes from Him; and that on which we nourish our flesh and blood, and which changes us, is the flesh and blood of Christ incarnate" (*Apol* 66,2). Each Christian is "washed with His blood who believes in Him and who receives through Him the remission of sins." Finally the power of Christ will be manifest in His *parousia* or second coming: "If I show such power has been given in the economy of His Passion," says Justin, "what will be His second coming in glory!" (*Dial* 31,1; 121,3). This will include the complete defeat of the demons so that those who believe in Him will be reunited in impassibility, incorruptibility, joy and immortality (*Dial* 45,4).

Toward the end of the second century, Irenaeus of Lyons, a disciple of Polycarp of Smyrna, who in turn knew St. John the Apostle, likewise presents his theology as an exposé of the common tradition. In his *Against All Heresies*, he explains the catechesis or doctrine of the faith in action, and organizes the traditional articles of the creed in such fashion as to show the Gnostic heretics, against whom in particular he is writing, the unity of God's design in the creation and redemption of man. He likewise uses the word *economy*, as does Justin, to describe the history of man's salvation as it was conceived before the beginning of time and worked out in the Passion, death and resurrection of Christ, and as it is now actuated in the Church. Irenaeus centers his theological thought on the notion of a recapitulation of all things in the God-Man, by whom all things have been created and who comes to regather all that is in His Incarnation. It is the Word of God who from the beginning modeled Adam in His image—the soul and spirit, not the body. In the course of the Old Testament, it was this same Christ who revealed God to man in the various theophanies; it cannot have been the Father since He is the invisible Creator, and cannot be contained in any part or even in the whole of the universe.

According to Irenaeus, Christ's coming down upon earth was aimed at bringing man up to God. Man, as born in the universe, was a child to be educated—and here the influence of the Greek pedagogy in the milieu in which he lives is obvious—under God's guidance. But as a child, man grew too eager and got out of hand, thus destroying the experiment whereby in complete liberty he was to be led by the hand of God to maturity; hence he had to be subjected to the Law of the Old Testament. Now Christ had come to give man more freedom, because what is done in freedom is greater and more honorable than the obsequiousness that is part of servitude. The Old and the New Testaments are thus two moments in man's existence, two successive types of education, and the step between them is occupied by man's salvation "in visible form."

The Incarnation is thus at the heart of the history of man's redemption, and Irenaeus expresses this phase of his thought again by the notion of recapitulation. In Greek rhetoric this word refers to the compendium of arguments in several chapters of a book. St. Paul uses it as meaning "bringing all things to a head in Christ." Finally, the word can have the meaning of "a reconstitution of all things once again" which seems to be the meaning of the Vulgate "*instaurare*."

In the death and resurrection of Christ Irenaeus sees at once the reconstitution in victory of all those who have preceded Him, prefiguring His words, sacrifices and deeds. But he also feels that Christ, as an infant, youth and man, has recapitulated the history of each individual, as well as of all mankind, and all are substantially saved in Christ. Further, in constituting the Church, Christ is the glorious head of His body, and the beginning of all spiritual life. He has thus recapitulated these things in Himself, uniting man with the Spirit and placing the

Spirit in man, and through man extending Himself throughout the entire expanse of creation.

In an age that witnessed fratricidal wars within the political continuum of the Roman Empire and was beginning to feel the pressure of the barbarian invasions, an age subject to a myriad of strange oriental, mystery religions, adding the confusion of Gnostic dualism to the superstition and cynical moral decadence already rampant in its greater cities, where the hopelessness of man's personal situation was vividly experienced, the temptation to despair was great and widespread, and the tendency to blame and wreak vengeance on a non-conformist group such as the new Christian sects was strong. This explains in part the sporadic outbreak of the anti-Christian persecution; but it also gives reason for the successful appeal of the Christian message which we see the Apologists and early theologians preaching in a manner capable of attracting and convincing many of their contemporaries. Justin and Irenaeus dig into the conscience of their age, and each in his own way offers it the message of true deliverance in the Redemption achieved for all by Christ.

Man's inner nature thus received considerable attention, and his difficulties in following the rules of right reason were traced as much to the obstacles and temptations put in his path by demons from without as by his ill humors from within. The weird descriptions of the devils that disturbed the peaceful wastes of the desert to which the early anchorites and hermits fled are a testimony of the self-conscious struggle for interior peace and the conquest of the passions to which these ascetics were devoted. It is doubtful whether the majority of these men and women were subject to the hallucinations so glibly ascribed to them by nineteenth-century literal-minded rationalists. But they did have a knowledge of the interior ills that afflicted them and described these disturbances in the biblical terms and atmosphere upon which their spirituality and the certitude of their redemption was founded. If Christ had been tempted by devils, there was all the more reason why they should be. And while in the East great emphasis was placed on man's destiny to return to the image and likeness of his Master—hence to achieve a type of divinization—it was precisely in this atmosphere that the greatest attention was given to the imitation of Christ in His sufferings. This in turn required a struggle with the Evil One, even in bodily form.

In the West, with Tertullian in particular and with Lactantius, demoniac influence is seen in every move of the pagan religious cult. Since the life of the ancient city was dominated by its gods, on every street, in all its temples, in its baths and public places, Tertullian could spy the presence of the devil. The emphasis in the Christian initiatory rites on exorcisms and on "renouncing Satan and all his works and pomps" was a natural reaction to this conviction, as was the insistence during times of persecution on a faithful abstention from sacrificing to the gods. In recompense, there was a guarantee that by His death on the Cross Christ had destroyed the power of Satan; and although there was always danger that the individual would betray himself into the situation described by Christ in the parable of the seven devils who returned to the soul swept and garnished by baptism to make that man's situation worse than before his conversion, this was part of the risk involved in the very idea of salvation.

There is then in the Church's theological tradition of the first four centuries a definite and purposeful pattern of adaptation: a recasting, dictated by the intellectual milieu, of the primary truths of salvation. All through the patristic age this endeavor will be manifest in the preaching of the word of God as fashioned and stimulated by the schools of thought at Carthage and Rome in the West, at Alexandria, Antioch, Edessa and Constantinople in the East. And each age produces its geniuses, from Tertullian and Cyprian, from Origen and Clement of Alexandria, to Hilary, Ambrose, Augustine and Leo, as well as to Basil, the Gregories, Cyril and John Chrysostom—men who not only engage in the theological controversies incident to the development of the Church's understanding of the great truths regarding the Trinity and the Incarnation, grace and the sacramental life, but who give specific attention to the philosophical and psychological problems of their day whereby, in their preaching and teaching, they can adapt the truths of faith and in particular the message of the Redemption to the personal needs of their audience.

II

The medieval world inherited from the ancient civilizations the habit of giving as much insight to inner subjective experience—in the form of religious inspiration, dreams, feelings, memories, anxieties, poetic, artistic and mythological hallucinations, selfish inner gratification, moral values, fears and aspirations—as it did to exterior activity and worldly accomplishments. The medieval man had no doubt about the existence of another world, and took the biblical account not only of creation, but of the existence of angels and devils, and of his own destiny between them, for "gospel truth." In fact, the medieval man, religious or otherwise, felt that man's final end was in some way aimed at the contemplation of the good, be it natural as expressed in truth and beauty, or supernatural in union with divine goodness and love. If he was tempted to despair it was not that there was nothing to be hopeful about, but simply that the immensity of supernatural reality, whose existence he head no reason to question, seemed so far beyond his capacity, as indicated by his poor capability in practicing virtue, that he might settle unhappily for the lot of the recreant in hell.

With the scientific certainty regarding natural phenomena introduced by Galileo and propagated by Descartes and the mathematicians in a mechanistic sense, not only were alchemy, astrology and occult science looked upon with askance, but gradually the old Greek *hubris* crept back into possession, and this time the seven devils of self-gratification were not exorcised as they had been by the ancient and medieval Church, but they were simply swept into a corner and denied existence. Rationalism could find no niche for them in the table of elements that constituted the physical universe; nor could their species and genus be categorized within the sphere of logical analysis, criteriology, or empirical psychology. So they were banished; and during the late nineteenth and early twentieth centuries, a devastating ridicule was poured upon the late Jewish and early Christian preoccupation with their existence and powers. The desert fathers, the makers of satanic gargoyles, and the purveyors of the mystery plays were looked upon as mountebanks, or what is worse, dispensers of diseased hallucinations.

With the devils, out went all necessity for the supernatural and all reference to the need for redemption. Man would be his own redeemer, conquering the earth and eventually dissecting the core of his own being by discovering the elements of life by test-tube analysis and group psychology. By the early 1900's Adam and Eve, original and actual sin, and compunction for guilt were described as atavistic hangovers that would disappear when modern education caught up with the cultural lag. But somehow this gap was never filled, and modern man felt himself tempted to despair of human nature the more he saw it employed in destructive drives such as war, genocide, and race and fraternal hatred.

III

Outside the stabilized religious societies, it is with Kierkegaard that modern man, at least in Western civilization, has come to some realization of his existence as a spoiled individual and a severely lonesome entity. Ridiculing what he called the ventriloquism of the philosopher, and reaching back to Socrates for inspiration, Kierkegaard attempted to return modern thought to the idea of individual salvation in Christ. Concentrating on man as an existing being, he found man juxtaposed between a consciousness of sin and a necessity of "grace" in the Christian significance of that word. He discovered three stages of existence: the esthetic, the ethical, and the religious, only to realize that while the esthetic crashes in doubt, the ethical bogs down in resignation or despair before the inevitability of death. Hence, there is meaningfulness only in the religious stage of existence.

It is thus with Kierkegaard that modern existential philosophy takes its rise, for he sees the concrete being that is man continually involved in a struggle with himself in the immediate now, painfully attempting to look forward, though actually he can only think backward. Only in this latter conviction is he at one with Hegel, whose Gnostic approach to the meaningfulness of Christianity leads him to conclude that only the backward-oriented side of man counts as real. With Jaspers there is an attempt to shake loose from the past and seek salvation in philosophy, although man's seemingly innate relation to transcendence is continually returning him to a consideration of religion. He feels, however, that Christianity has been destroyed by its dogmas, cult and law, and that Christ is actually the hero of the negative, since He failed to participate in the worldly engagements of culture, politics and family life. Yet he is haunted by the fact that the Bible as an existential experience is stronger than philosophy.

Meanwhile, however, Freud, Adler and Jung arrived on the scene and, following the lead of nineteenth-century pioneers in the psychology of man's interior underworld, drove exploratory shafts below the emotional and conscious surface of human intelligence to discover unchartered depths and murk-filled caverns within the psyche which they hesitated to call the soul. It was here, of course, that Freud found the libido, perhaps because he did not know what else to look for; whereas Jung was willing to acknowledge the more diversified drives summed up in the seven capital sins. Once the lid was lifted on the psyche, however, out came the seven demons bringing with them seven more dastardly than the original. Thus contemporary man has had good reason for the despair that has expressed itself in the silence of alienation, atheistic existentialism, and the final, infantile disdain for meaning in the arts. What is now vociferously denied is not so much a heaven or hell as the very concept of significance.

To stem this avalanche, Gabriel Marcel made an attempt to face the existentialism of the hour with a Christian accommodation, and to demonstrate the Christian adaptability of love, truth, faith and hope by an absolute engagement against hatred, betrayal, agnosticism and doubt. The highest form of this adaptability of the Christian message is the I-and-You relation between God and man, and it has been demonstrated undeniably in the Incarnation of the God–Man, Jesus Christ.

In imitation of or in reaction to Marcel, a number of Christian theologians and thinkers began to face once again the acute existentialist problems of modern man. And it is into the present chaos of man's existence that the Catholic Church, with Vatican Council II, is preparing to plunge, bearing the good news of the Redemption. But it has become aware that there is nothing so banal as the very expression "good news"; and, with difficulty, it is beginning to see that the mechanistic and rational explanations of the truths of the faith, which it unconsciously took over from the spirit of the age just past, are now not only inadequate but actually meaningless to modern man. On this plane, what Vatican Council II has proven thus far is that many good and intelligent churchmen are actually afraid of the mysteries of the faith, the cultivation of the charismatic gifts that characterized the early Church, and the admission that a rational approach in apologetics and

a mechanistic carrying out of the sacraments and cere-
monies could possibly be unconvincing to the reasonable
man.

IV

In a world inhabited by the devils of the unconscious as
well as the demons of nuclear destruction, there is only one
hope, and that is in the Cross of Calvary on which the
Son of God broke the power of Satan and redeemed all of
mankind. The theology of the Redemption begins with
the Trinity which in turn is knowable only through the
mystery of the Incarnation: Christ who is God, giving
witness to the fact that in the God with whom all begins,
is and ends, there is an infinite love that is not enjoyed by
only One, but shared equally by Three Persons; and that
these Three Persons so loved the work of creation, and
modern as well as ancient man, that the Second Person was
willing to obey the Father, empty Himself, and take upon
Himself human flesh and mortality within the context of
a world besmirched with human sinfulness.

It is this incredible fact that the early Christians got
across to ancient man, and which was accepted almost un-
questioningly by medieval man, at least in one quarter of
the world. But medieval man did not hesitate to take over
likewise the mystical and emotional elements that are part
of this message of salvation, and which fill the sermons
and books of theologians and preachers from Peter the
Venerable to Thomas Aquinas and Bernardine of Siena.

The problem before the modern Christian is to rephrase
this message and rearrange the incidence of this fact so

that it may meet the minds of an unhinged generation. The word of God was meant for twentieth-century man as immediately as it was for first or fourteenth-century man, and grace has a healing and restorative power for the psychotic and neurotic ills of today, more particularly when they are now being laid open by the scalpel of modern psychology and psychiatry. What is perhaps even more important is a reworking of the message so that its meaning may be clear to the half-educated and fairly well educated to whom the elucidation of personality, family and community tensions, in the form of labeled anxieties, is being directed daily in novels, the theatre, television, radio and newspapers, not to mention high school and college classrooms.

The ordinary Catholic and Christian believes well enough in the message of Redemption, at least when he says the *Credo* and participates in a religious ceremony. But for the most part he is completely unaware of its relevance to his job, his home, or his position in society on a level where he can do something about it without being considered a religious fanatic. It is here that the real challenge is now offered to Christianity. If the significance of the Redemption can be made meaningful and actual at this ground level, the hope is justified that it can be utilized in the below-surface areas of the obviously distraught and dislocated.

What this implies is a new ordination of the Christian mysteries which is being hinted at in the discusson on the nature of the Church and approached in the Constitution on the Liturgy at the Council. But this is far from sufficient. There is only one permanent way of banishing the seven devils, and that is with the fire of the Holy Spirit that Christ came to cast upon the earth. It does not mean burning the house down, nor scorching out of existence the people playing with the fires of human passion and anxieties on a purely natural plane. It does mean lighting up the dark places of human understanding and projecting Christ before modern man as "the Light of the world" in such fashion that His redemptive graces will reach the foul pit inhabited by the avaricious and power-hungry, the adulterers and pornographers, the sick of soul and body, as well as the unheeding who make up that vast multitude of sinners whom Christ said He came to save! Since there is much more to man than meets the eye, every form of grace must be welcomed, even should it take on aspects that appear unscientific or unreasonable in the context of the twentieth-century worship of Mammon.

In imitation of the Fathers of the first centuries of the Church, who in turn were intent upon the imitation of Christ, the function of the Church today is to adapt the message of salvation for "a doctrinal penetration and a formation of consciences in faithful and perfect conformity to authentic doctrine, which, however, should be studied and expounded through the methods of research and through the literary forms of modern thought." This can only be done by meeting existentialistic man in his own milieu and convincing him that there is Redemption in the Son of God whose name and definition of Himself is "I am who am!"

The Moral Obligation of Obeying the Papal Encyclicals

▶▶

DANIEL LOWERY, C.SS.R., Ph.D.

In recent years, and especially since *Humani Generis* of Pope Pius XII, theologians have focused a good deal of attention on problems relevant to the doctrinal value or doctrinal authority of the papal encyclicals.[1] The purpose here is to attempt to assemble the more significant theological views into an organized whole. We do not intend to be original. The value, if any, will be in the line of organization rather than in the line of speculative investigation.

The first, and seemingly most difficult, question that one must grapple with is this: Does the teaching contained in papal encyclicals fall under the *extraordinary* or *ordinary* teaching power of the Roman Pontiff? Several surveys of theological manuals and specialized studies [2] indicate that there has not been unanimity of teaching, or at least not unanimity of expression, on this question. In an excellent article the late Edward D. Benard pursued this question at considerable length. The position adopted by Fr. Benard appears eminently sound and workable. Moreover, despite the inevitable nominal variations, it seems to include within itself the teachings of the vast majority of contemporary theologians.[3]

Fr. Benard summarized his own position in three propositions:

1. "The Pope employs his extraordinary magisterium when he speaks *ex cathedra*. This extraordinary magisterium is *de se*, always, and necessarily infallible."[4] On this proposition there seems to be no real difference of opinion among Catholic theologians. The Vatican definition surely means that "speaking infallibly" and speaking "*ex cathedra*" are two ways of describing the same act. Both expressions indicate that the Pope has fulfilled the four conditions outlined in the Vatican definition. "The fulfillment of the conditions equals an *ex cathedra* pronouncement equals the fulfillment of the conditions; or in any sequential arrangement that can be made of the three elements."[5] The term *ex cathedra* is the pivotal term in an effort to discuss the ordinary and extraordinary teaching powers of the Roman Pontiff. The proposition stated by Fr. Benard seems very sound precisely because his starting point is the Vatican definition. According to the definition, an *ex cathedra* pronouncement can be equated with an infallible pronouncement. "If we go beyond the Vatican definition, and maintain that non-*ex cathedra* pronouncements may sometimes be infallible, we are opening up a 'shadow-zone' that has no limits but the theologians' opinion of its extent."[6] Fr. Benard did not, of course, exclude the possibility of further definitions on papal infallibility, but in the *present* state of defined doctrine it is justifiable, and preferable, to equate "ex cathedra pro-

nouncement and infallible pronouncement." Naturally, when the Pope speaks *ex cathedra*, his definition obliges the whole Church to consent.

2. "The Pope employs his ordinary magisterium when he speaks to the faithful, indeed as their supreme pastor and teacher, but in order to expound, explain, present Catholic teaching, or to admonish, persuade, enlighten, warn and encourage the faithful; without calling upon the supreme exercise of his apostolic authority and without, in the strict sense, defining a doctrine. In this case he does not speak *ex cathedra* and the ordinary magisterium is hence not *de se* infallible."[7]

This proposition seems to express quite clearly what is meant by the ordinary magisterium of the Pope. Some theologians, as shall be pointed out later, are at pains to show that the ordinary teaching of the Pope is not as subject to error as that of other scholars and theologians.

3. "However, the Pope may, if he chooses, employ a usual organ or vehicle of the ordinary magisterium as the medium of an *ex cathedra* pronouncement."[8] Until now, as far as this writer knows, the Popes have never used an encyclical letter, in the strict sense, to define a doctrine of faith and morals. Recent Popes have, however, used a more formal document, the papal constitution, for this purpose. In this third proposition, Fr. Benard is simply emphasizing the truth that the Pope *could* use an encyclical letter to make known a solemn definition. The Pope is free to use any vehicle or organ he chooses. It is altogether possible that he may, at some future date, take advantage of world-wide television to broadcast a solemn definition to the world. There is certainly no intrinsic reason why encyclical

letters have not, so far, contained infallible definitions of faith and morals.

Some theologians, while no doubt agreeing substantially with the propositions stated above, are at pains to prevent certain possible misunderstandings. First of all, some point out that in the course of an encyclical, which is not *de se* infallible, the Pope may restate certain divinely revealed doctrines, or doctrines defined infallibly by the Church at some previous date. For example, in an encyclical on marriage the Pope may state that marriage is a sacrament. Obviously, the Pope is not defining this doctrine; it was previously defined by the Council of Trent. The fact that the Pope is using his ordinary teaching power in the encyclical as a whole does not, of course, mean that doctrines previously defined lose any of their original authority. It seems curious, however, that theologians would stoutly attribute infallibility to the ordinary magisterium "on the mere grounds that in it the Pope may *repeat* something already infallibly true on other, previous grounds"; for "when anyone, even the famous 'simple theologian' repeats an infallible statement he is stating something infallibly true." [9]

Other theologians, and for a more substantive reason, put special emphasis on the fact that the Pope, even when using his ordinary teaching power, receives special help and assistance from the Holy Spirit. The general argument is that Almighty God would never allow the Pope to make a serious mistake in teaching the universal Church. If the Vicar of Christ on earth is to fulfill his divinely appointed task of guiding men safely and surely to eternal salvation, he must receive from God necessary protection against serious and official error. In this regard a statement of Pope Pius XI is significant:

> It is quite foreign to everyone bearing the name of Christian to hold that they must obey only in those matters which she the Church has decreed by solemn definition, as though her other decisions might be presumed false or insufficiently grounded in truth and moral righteousness . . . A characteristic of all true followers of Christ, lettered or unlettered, is to allow themselves to be guided and led, in all things that touch upon faith and morals, by the holy Church of God through its supreme pastor the Roman Pontiff, who *is himself guided by Jesus Christ our Lord*. . . .[10]

Joseph C. Fenton sums up what would seem to be a common theological view on this point:

> To the Holy Father's responsibility of caring for the sheep of Christ's fold, there corresponds, on the part of the Church's membership, the basic obligation of following his directions, in doctrinal as well as disciplinary matters. In this field, God has given the Holy Father *a kind of infallibility* distinct from the charism of doctrinal infallibility in the strict sense. He has so constructed and ordered the Church that those who follow the directives given to the entire kingdom of God on earth will never be brought into the position of ruining themselves spiritually through this obedience. Our Lord dwells within His Church in such a way that those who obey the disciplinary and doctrinal directives of this society can never find themselves displeasing God through their adherence to the teachings and the commands given to the universal Church militant.[11]

In answer to the first question: Does the teaching contained in papal encyclicals fall under the extraordinary or ordinary teaching power of the Roman Pontiffs?, it may be said this teaching normally falls under the ordinary teaching power. The encyclicals are generally vehicles of authentic, but not infallible, papal teaching. This is not to say that encyclicals could not contain new *ex cathedra* pronouncements; nor does this mean that none of the teaching contained in encyclicals could be characterized as infallible. The point is that the Popes ordinarily do not use encyclicals to define new doctrine. The Catholic, therefore, is not obliged to accept the ordinary teachings of the encyclicals as doctrines of divine or ecclesiastical faith.

This conclusion brings us to a second question. If the non-infallible teachings of the encyclicals do not demand the assent of faith, what kind of an assent, if any, do they demand? That the teachings contained in the encyclicals do demand assent of some kind is beyond question. Even before *Humani Generis*, "there was one point on which all theologians" were manifestly in agreement. They were "all convinced that all Catholics are bound in conscience to give a definite internal religious assent to those doctrines which the Holy Father teaches when he speaks to the universal Church of God on earth without employing his God-given charism of infallibility," [12] In *Humani Generis* Pope Pius XII clearly asserted that the teachings of the encyclicals demand a response from the Catholic. "It must not be thought that what is expounded in encyclical letters does not of itself demand consent, since in writing such letters the Popes do not exercise the supreme power of their teaching authority. For these matters are taught with the ordinary teaching authority, of which it is true to say: 'He who hears you, hears Me'; and generally what is expounded and inculcated in encyclical letters already for other reasons pertains to Catholic doctrine." [13] Thus, the Pope insists that encyclicals, besides often containing matters of dogma, teach matters which demand of themselves a positive assent on the part of the faithful.

What is the nature of the assent due to the teachings of the encyclicals? Fr. Benard remarks that there "are three general classes of assent involved when we speak of reception of the teachings of the magisteria of the Church and the Pope." [14] Not all theologians agree [15] and even those who agree that there are three classes do not agree on terminology. Fr. Benard's classification is as follows: 1) *divine and Catholic faith*, by which we believe those things that are contained in Sacred Scripture or the apostolic tradition and are proposed to us as divinely revealed, either by the Church's solemn (extraordinary) or ordinary magisterium, or by the Sovereign Pontiff speaking *ex cathedra*; 2) *fides mediate divina* (sometimes called "fides ecclesiastica"), by which we assent to those truths which are not in themselves revealed, but which are connected with revelation, that is, their accurate teaching is necessary for the integral presentation and protection of the revealed truths; 3) *internal religious assent*, which is the assent we give to non-infallible utterances, including those expounded in the encyclicals. The term "religious assent" seems to be the most common among modern theologians,[16] but the terms "pious assent" or "obediential consent" are sometimes seen.

The assent is, first of all, a *religious* assent. "It is truly religious by reason of its object and motives." [17] "Even where infallibility is not involved, nevertheless our assent . . . does ultimately depend upon our faith in the teaching authority of the Vicar of Christ on earth. We assent *as Catholics*; with the humility and docility and wholeheartedness proper to a religious act."[18]

Concerning the assent given, certain distinctions are in order. It is possible that the Pope may propose a truth for which there is real intrinsic evidence. It is equally possible that the Catholic, especially after serious reflection, may "see" the force of the evidence, may understand its probative value. In this case the assent given "is characterized as knowledge." [19] Such assent will ordinarily cause no difficulty.

It is also possible that the Pope may propose a truth for which there does not seem to be any real intrinsic evidence; or at least an individual Catholic may be unable to perceive the force of the evidence. These truths demand assent from the Catholic. The assent in this case is really an "act of belief"; the assent is given on *extrinsic* grounds. This act of belief is not, however, an unreasonable or irrational act. It is, in fact, "a way of attaining truth that otherwise could not be attained; for when intrinsic evidence is lacking . . . there is no road by which we can arrive at truth except the road of belief." [20] The extrinsic grounds on which the assent is based may be characterized as "the authority and doctrinal competence of the supreme teacher of Christendom." [21]

Further, it is possible that the Pope may propose in encyclicals what can only be called matters of opinion. Opinion, of course, does not include certitude about the proposition proposed; opinion necessarily involves "fear of the opposite." Fr. Benard asks: "What constitutes, exactly, the 'internal religious assent' that we elicit in a matter of opinion?" His answer is wonderfully clear:

I think it is twofold. As regards the opinion itself, we do not, of course, have certitude that what the proposition states is true. If we did have that certitude, we would no longer be in the field of opinion, and it is precisely as an opinion that the matter is presented to us. Motivated by the authority and competency of the Holy Father, we hold the matter precisely *as an opinion* . . .

I believe, however, that there is something more than this required for the integral unconditional internal assent we owe to the Pontifical statement even in the field of opinion. We also assent unconditionally, with no fear of error, to the fact that the opinion the Pope sets forth is *well founded* and safe, and is the opinion that we as Catholics are to act upon and follow.[22]

It has already been stated that this "religious assent" must be truly internal. It is a true internal act, "not a mere silentium obsequium such as the Jansenists were willing to give the papal decrees issued against them."[23] The practical implications of the "internalness" of this assent are summarized well by Thomas Harte, C.SS.R., when he says: "Once the Pope has spoken, a mere external conformity, or 'keeping an open mind' attitude, ceases to be possible. Catholics must yield both judgment and will to the teaching authority of the Church, even though they may not completely understand a principle or directive unequivocally stated by the Holy See. Obedience to the Vicar of Chirst is imperative for all the faithful."[24]

It would seem obvious that this internal assent must perdure as long as the papal proposition remains the same. It is possible, and has in fact happened, that the Popes will modify a position on some details which have been presented in an encyclical letter. This may be especially true in the socio-economic encyclicals. But the internal assent would be obligatory until the Popes themselves modify the teaching previously presented. The fact that some people *think* the position should be modified would hardly justify the withholding of assent.

In *Humani Generis*, after asserting that matters expounded in encyclical letters do demand consent, Pius XII went on to state another principle of great importance: "But if the Supreme Pontiffs in their official documents purposely pass judgment on a matter up to that time under dispute, it is obvious that the matter, according to the mind and will of the same Pontiffs, cannot be any longer considered a question open to discussion among theologians." [25] The key phrase here is the "purposely pass judgment," *data opera sententiam ferunt*. After a careful study of the *data opera*, Fr. Benard concludes: "I think it is safe to say that a *data opera* statement is one made with express intention and clear, positive application; it is the result of previous direct deliberation; it is not casual or incidental; it is not an *obiter dictum*." [26] The second part of the phrase *sententiam ferunt* receives this commentary from Fr. Benard: "Considering the whole background, aura, and connotation of the phrase *"sententiam ferre,"* I suggest that it means more than just any direct statement; it connotes something in the nature of a measured, decisive judgment with regard to some controversial point." [27]

John Ford, S.J. and Gerald Kelly, S.J. although primarily interested in the *moral* pronouncements of the Holy See, emphasize what Fr. Benard hints at: namely, if a non-infallible papal pronouncement is going to close a controversy among theologians, *the decisive character of the pronouncement must be evident.*[28] But it is one thing to say that the decisive character of the document must be evident, and quite another to make a practical judgment about particular statements of the Holy See. What is really necessary is *sound interpretation* of papal documents by competent theologians.

There can be no doubt that interpretation is truly necessary; yet there does not exist an official set of norms for the interpretation of papal documents. In fact, the whole question of how to interpret papal documents seems to need a good deal of investigation. However, it is possible to decide on certain basic norms of interpretation that are in conformity with the mind and practice of the Holy See.

One such norm would be a close study of the *verbal formulas used*. W. J. Smith, S.J., in his article "How To Interpret Papal Documents," places first emphasis on the study of the actual meaning of the words used. He adds that "the solemnity of the terms employed in the documents must also be studied." [29] Ford and Kelly, while agreeing that the verbal formulas used are very important, wisely point out that "the words themselves are not the ultimate criterion of the true sense of the papal pronouncement; they can be obscure and admit of reformulation." [30]

To get to the true sense, the theologian must study not only the words, but *the context* as well. It is imperative that the documents "be placed in the historical and local context of their production." [31] Ford and Kelly state:

> By the context we mean not so much the verbal context as the historical setting, because it is there particularly that we are apt to find the true meaning of the statement. For example, if the Pope is settling a controversy, his words should be taken in conjunction with the contro-

versy; if he is condemning an error, the words should be interpreted with reference to the error and so forth.[32]

In accord with sound methods of historical criticism, both the study of the words and the study of the context will be greatly facilitated by an investigation of the *sources* used in the preparation of the document. These can throw light on the meanings of words, on the historical and scientific presuppositions of the documents, and therefore on the type of judgment or decision contained in the papal pronouncement.[33]

It is hoped that these few pages have served to organize some of the more important recent theological reflection on the place of papal encyclicals in Catholic theology. Encyclicals will no doubt play a large role in the continuing teaching of the Roman Pontiffs for years to come.

NOTES

[1] What is said here of encyclicals may be applied to the whole range of the ordinary magisterium of the Holy Father. It would apply, therefore, to radio messages, allocutions, and the like.

[2] See especially Joseph C. Fenton, "The Doctrinal Authority of Papal Encyclicals," *Amer. Eccles. Review* (1949), pp. 136-150, 210-220. E. D. Benard, "The Doctrinal Value of the Ordinary Teaching of the Holy Father in View of *Humani Generis*," *Proceedings* (1951), pp. 78-109.

[3] Benard admits that Dublonchy and Billot did not agree with him.

[4] Benard, *loc. cit.*, p. 84.

[5] *Ibid.*, p. 80.

[6] *Ibid.*, p. 108.

[7] *Ibid.*, p. 84. Also Cotter, *The Encyclical Humani Generis*, 1951. Thomas Peques, "L'autorité des encycliques pontificales," *Revue Thomiste* (1904), pp. 512-32.

[8] *Ibid.*, p. 85.

[9] *Ibid.*, p. 86.

[10] Pius XI, *Casti Connubi*, #103.

[11] Fenton, *loc. cit.*, p. 144.

[12] *Ibid.*, p. 144.

[13] *Humani Generis*, p. 20.

[14] Benard, *loc. cit.*, p. 91.

[15] *E.g.* C. Journet, *The Church of the Word Incarnate* (New York: Sheed, 1955), p. 352.

[16] Fenton, *loc. cit.*, p. 136.

[17] *Ibid.*, p. 147.

[18] Benard, *loc. cit.*, p. 98.

[19] *Ibid.*, p. 92.

[20] *Ibid.*, p. 94. "May I repeat that our assent to the teaching of the ordinary magisterium is a fitting act of reasonable men because of the authority and the competence of the Teacher who proposes the truth to be believed. Our belief is fundamentally a rational act and a justified act; any charges of "intellectual tyranny" are just so much nonsense." (p. 96)

[21] *Ibid.*, p. 96.

[22] *Ibid.*, p. 98.

[23] Cotter, p. 75.

[24] Thomas J. Harte, C.SS.R., *Papal Social Principles* (Bruce, 1956), p. 13.

[25] *Humani Generis*, #20.

[26] Benard, *loc. cit.*, p. 101.

[27] *Ibid.*, p. 102.

[28] John Ford, S.J. and Gerald Kelly, S.J., *Contemporary Moral Theology* (Newman, 1958), p. 32.

[29] W. J. Smith, S.J., "How To Interpret Papal Documents," *Catholic Mind* (Feb., 1962), p. 21.

[30] Ford and Kelly, *op. cit.*, p. 29. "This can be illustrated by the acta of both Pius XI and Pius XII relative to punitive sterilization, as well as by the tenor of canon law and by the reactions of eminent theologians to certain aspects of significant moral pronouncements."

[31] Smith, *loc. cit.*, p. 21.

[32] Ford and Kelly, *op. cit.*, p. 31.

[33] Smith, *loc. cit.*, p. 21. Smith stresses two other rules that should be kept in mind in interpreting papal documents: 1) "The documents must be considered against the totality of Catholic teaching, as it has unfolded over the centuries"; and 2) "The teaching of a pope who has reigned for a fair number of years often shows a certain continuity and development, and this factor should be taken into account in reading any new document issued by the same person."

Communism and Internationalism

JOHN LERHINAN, C.SS.R., Ph.D.

From its very origin, in the time of Marx, Communism was in essence, international. It was for a group known as the League of the Communists that Karl Marx wrote the Manifesto of the Communist Party—not for a Communist Party such as we know it today.

At that time there was a League of Communists in London, Paris, Brussels, Hungary, Germany, Austria, Switzerland, etc. It is evident that this League of Communists for whom Marx and Engels wrote the Manifesto of the Communist Party should not be confused with the organization known as the First International Workingmen's Association. For the first Congress of the League of Communists took place in London in 1847 whereas the First International Workingmen's Association was not organized until Sept. 28, 1864.

The great importance that Marx and Engels attached to internationalism is clear from the text of the Manifesto. It is especially in the final section of that work that emphasis is placed on the international character of the movement. After discussing the conditions of Communists and opposition parties in England, France, Germany, Poland, etc. it concludes by saying that "in short the Communists everywhere support every revolutionary movement." Then there follows the slogan that has been heard around the world: Workingmen of all countries, unite!

There is, therefore, embedded in modern Communism from its very beginning, the idea and policy of internationalism.

According to Marx the basis of this internationalism was the international character of the capitalistic system. The League of Communists, consequently, identified itself with the proletariat especially under the aspect of workingmen who were exploited by the system. It followed, then, that they had an interest in all countries where capitalism existed.

The very name of the organization founded in 1864 under the title of The First International Workingmen's Association indicated that the Communists were planning to overcome the limits of nationalism. At the meeting during which it originated at St. Martin's Hall in London a committee was appointed to work out a program for this International and to call a subsequent International Congress to approve the program and statutes. This committee was international in character: it included Frenchmen, Italians, Poles, Englishmen, Swiss and Germans.

It was at this first meeting that Karl Marx gave the Inaugural Address, and again concluded his remarks, after placing great stress upon fraternity and international organization, with a slogan that had been used previously: Workers of the World, Unite!

It is interesting to note that, in the beginning at least,

Marx and Engels insisted that all should have equal rights in this International. Likewise it is interesting to see that within a very few years when the suggestion was made that Russians might occupy important places in the sections of the International, Engels wrote to Marx and complained that the Russians will insinuate themselves into leading positions and bring the private intrigues and squabbles which are inseparable from them, thus creating a great problem for the International.

Actually this First International did not succeed in decreasing the strength of nationalism among the workers and it showed itself to be very ineffectual at the time of its great crisis in the Franco-Prussian War of 1870.

The International suffered a very severe setback in 1871 when it supported the Paris Commune. The Commune was crushed by the French Government which not only punished severely those involved but also encouraged the other European Powers to take stern measures against the International.

The next Congress which was held in the autumn of 1872 brought a new problem in the form of a powerful opposition group led by Bakunin, a Russian. He was actually an anarchist who demanded the abolition of all classes and all forms of authority. Marx opposed him and managed to have him expelled from the International.

The First International lasted only a few years more. It was moved to the United States and was dissolved by a resolution passed at a meeting in Philadelphia in July 1876.

An examination of the history of the League of Communists and the First International brings out certain ideas that have remained permanently prominent in modern

Communism. There is the insistence, first of all, upon an internationalism which arises from the "fact" of common exploitation of workers in many parts of the world. There is the tendency to talk in terms of working people and to use language which pictures real or imaginary injustices. Promises are made that these injustices will be corrected if the program of Communism is accepted and followed. Finally there is within the Communist organization the conflict between its two extreme factions which always seem to be present: the left wing insisting upon immediate, violent direct action for the overthrow of the enemies of Communism and the seizing of power, and the right wing led by Marx and supported by those Communists who have not actually come into power in Russia and many of the other countries. These favor a policy of gradualism. They want to build up the basis for the eventual construction of Communism. They want to effect a gradual change in people's outlook on the meaning of life. For, said Marx, people must be given time to change themselves and during that time organized Communism can work to change the political and economic international situation.

Thirteen years were to pass between the end of the First International and the beginning of the Second. During that period there were a large number of international Socialist Congresses which were evidence of the fact that the working class had not abandoned the idea of collaboration on the international plane. However, there was no permanent organization for such activity.

It was on the occasion of a celebration of the one hundred anniversary of the French Revolution, July 14, 1889 that the Second International was organized in Paris. It was composed of two groups: the non-Marxists who, for the most part represented strict trade-union interests from the various nations, and the Marxists. The Second International adopted some of Marx's basic principles, namely, the class struggle, international unity of the proletariat and the socialization of the means of production, though even these principles were interpreted differently by the two groups.

From the beginning the non-Marxists were the larger group but the Marxists were willing to join with them in the hope of reaching many workers who were not Marxist and also with the idea of eventually gaining control of the organization.

However, other changes were taking place which made it impossible for the Marxists to achieve their goal. In many countries parliamentary democracy was being established and the working class parties were able to get a large number of their members into the Parliaments. Thus they had the means of presenting their demands for social improvements in their own countries and of working through legitimate channels to bring these about. In many instances, therefore, especially in regard to Germany, France, and England, there was no more need of having recourse to the International to reach these goals. Besides, economic and social conditions in Western Europe gradually began to improve. The workingman benefitted both from wage increases and social reforms. These factors also made it very difficult for an international radical organization to gain support.

One of the interesting facts about the Second Interna-

tional is that we find in it the different schools of interpretation of Communist teachings which will reappear in
present-day Communism, namely Reformism and Revisionism. Reformism consisted in adhering to the abstract formulas of Marxism while working for improvements within
the present social system. The Revisionists, on the other
hand, maintained that some of the principles of Marx were
erroneous so that international proletarian organizations did
not have to follow all of his teachings. Among the Revisionists, we can mention Edward Bernstein who denied
Marx's theory of surplus value and also Marx's belief in
the impending collapse of the capitalist system.

As in the First International, so also in the Second, the
Anarchists caused a great deal of difficulty and were eventually expelled from the organization in 1896. Nevertheless
the First International had a more genuine revolutionary
trend than the Second even though there was disagreement as to the methods to be used to attain its ends. The
Second International was really an assembly of Workers
Organizations which were loosely tied together and represented varying degrees of maturity and different shades of
Socialist opinion. Nor was the Second International as
centralized as the First. There the delegates were chosen
at its own congresses but in the Second the delegates represented other autonomous groups, such as trade-unions, and
they were bound by the mandates of these groups. As a
result the Second International possessed very slight disciplinary powers and was in this sense a very weak organization.

The Second International died during the First World
War. Its dissolution was caused by a number of factors:

its structural weakness, the violent clashes between many of its leaders as, for example, Lenin and Kautsky, the misconceptions as to the international solidarity of workers, tremendous influence of nationalism, the inability of the organization to have a strong program with clearly defined goals and precise principles.

As for Lenin, while he took part in the deliberations of the Second International from time to time, he never played a leading role perhaps because many of his ideas received little support. When the organization collapsed, therefore, he did not call for its revival but was already working on plans for a new organization to take its place. His views were made public particularly at the most important internationalist Socialist conference of the war years near Bern, Switzerland from Sept. 5 to 8, 1915. Even here he did not receive a majority in favor of his ideas though his support was larger than what he had in the Second International. Among his allies were Trotsky, Zinoviev and Radek who were to become famous in a few years.

The real importance of this conference arose from the fact that this was the first time that Lenin was able to attract a large number of adherents to his position and to extend his influence among the German Socialists, even among those who were to the left and to the right of him.

Almost as soon as he returned to Russia Lenin began to demand the establishment of the Third International. In April, 1917 he said: "Our Party must not wait but must immediately found a Third International." Because of his conviction that an all-European revolution was coming and that he possessed the right strategy and tactics for handling the situation, he insisted (and in this he was supported by the Russian Communist Party) on keeping himself aloof from any attempt to revive the Second International.

When he initiated the Third International, he experienced some difficulty in getting it to commence its work. Finally, however, on March 2, 1919, 51 Communists from 30 countries attended the First World Congress of the Third International in Moscow. Most of these delegates had already been in Russia. However, there were independent Communist Parties in Latvia, Finland, Hungary, Austria, etc. so the Russian Party did not have complete control over the meetings as was the case in Stalin's later years. The fact is that despite Lenin's plan it was doubtful for some time whether a new organization would be established permanently by the delegates. And there originally was no intention of leaving the executive organ of the International in Moscow. Moscow was considered to be its temporary home and the idea was to move it to Berlin as soon as a German Soviet Republic would be established. Moreover, many of the delegates hoped that with the arrival of representatives of the non-Russian Parties the comrades belonging to the country where the executive organ was located would not continue to have so much influence and perform so much of the work of that important body.

The constitution of the Third International was not decided upon at this first congress. There was an executive committee created and the Communist Parties of Russia, Germany, Austria, Hungary, the Balkan Confederation, Switzerland and the Scandinavian area were to send one delegate each to this committee. In the light of such background and the strength of the revolutionary movements in other countries at this time, we can understand why it was that the Russian Communist Party did not have complete control though it did play a very important part in the Comintern up until 1924 at which time it gained complete control.

It is true that, as Borkenau has pointed out, the work of preparing for the new International was done in the Ministry of Foreign Affairs of the Soviet Union so that it is evident that the Russians wished to use the organization as a means of implementing their foreign policy. It is also true that Lenin used the congress as an occasion for announcing the principles that were to guide the work of the Third International so that it would be following the dictates of the Communist Party of the Soviet Union. It was for this reason that the basic documents of this congress were worked out by the best brains of the Soviet Party as Nollau has pointed out. They included the guiding principles of the international Communist Congress by Bukarhin, the thesis on bourgeois democracy and proletarian dictatorship by Lenin, and the Manifesto of the Communist International to the proletariats of the world composed by Trotsky.

Zinoviev, who was then Lenin's right-hand man, was elected President of the International and through him, Lenin exercised a great influence upon the movement. Angelica Balabanova who was at the time a member of the supreme body of the Comintern reported that many of the agents were chosen because they had no interest in the labor movement and were, therefore, ready to obey the most outrageous and contradictory orders. Moreover, they departed from Russia with large sums of money on secret missions and were received as the representatives of Moscow by sympathetic workers' organizations in other countries.

Zinoviev, Bukarhin and Radek formed the day-to-day leadership of the Third International and Trotsky also joined in the activities of the organization especially where France was concerned. Still it is clear from the article that Zinoviev wrote in the first issue of the Comintern periodical that he expected a number of Communist Parties to gain control of their own governments and that their representatives in the Comintern would then be independent of Moscow. However, the Communist governments in Bavaria and Hungary lasted only a very short time while in Germany and Italy the Party, though it had many opportunities and grew quite strong, was never able to gain control of the government and soon suffered severe setbacks.

Nevertheless by 1920 the Comintern acquired a large following and a great deal of sympathy among the working classes of Europe especially in France, Germany, Italy and England. One reason for its growth was that it was not as yet completely under the domination of the Russian Party.

The Second World Congress of the Third International Workingmen's Association or Comintern was held from July 19 to August 7, 1920. By this time the Bolsheviks had won the Civil War and the Red Army was advancing in the direction of Warsaw. The Bolsheviks hoped to move west and unite with the German proletariat and thus bring about revolution in the whole of Western Europe. The Executive Committee, therefore, in sending out invitations for this congress emphasized the idea that the time had now come to organize the Communist proletariat and to make a serious effort to start the revolution. It is interesting to note that not only Communist Parties and red trade-unions were invited to take part in these meetings, but also Communist women's organizations and Communist youth organizations. It is still Communist policy to have front organizations for the women and youth groups.

There were many more delegates at this Congress than at the first one. Most of them represented Communist Parties but there were representatives also from some non-Communist Parties. The first meeting took place in Smolny in Russia near Petrograd which had been the headquarters of the October Revolution. There was a noticeable increase of Russian influence as compared to the First Congress of the Comintern though there was still freedom of discussion.

One of the central policies agreed upon was the one laid down by Lenin in his Leftwing Communism, namely that compromise very often should be used. This agreement was reached despite the fact that one faction wanted to be more belligerent.

Still the main idea of the Congress was to organize the Comintern in such a way that its member parties would be no longer independent parties but rather sections of a single world Communist Party. With this in mind the Congress gave to the Executive Committee a degree of power that was far greater than that possessed by any organ in the Second International. Later on this power passed over to the Central Committee of the Communist

Party of the Soviet Union and the Secret Police and they were able to use this power over foreign Communists very effectively.

While there was some doubt as to where the Executive Committee would be permanently located, the Soviets suggested that the country which was host to the Comintern should have five representatives on this Committee. Actually it did remain in Moscow and this was one of the means the Soviets used to get control of it. In addition, Karl Radek was considered to be the representative of Poland though for years he has been working for the Russians. Moreover, the representatives of the trade-unions and youth organizations were also from Russia.

The principle of organization in the Comintern was known as "democratic centralism" which meant that the member parties must submit to the decisions of the Executive Committee even in regard to what would normally be considered their own internal affairs. An interesting example of the conflict between the authority of the Executive Committee and the desires of an individual national Communist Party took place in 1938 when the Polish Communist Party was dissolved by a resolution of the Executive Committee in Moscow. The desire of Polish Communists to be freed from domination by their Moscow comrades was to manifest itself again many years later and in a very dramatic way.

Another important topic at this Second World Congress of the Third International was the conditions in the colonial areas of the world. There was agreement that the struggle had to be carried on there against the reactionary influence of priests and Christian missionaries. Likewise it was decided to oppose Pan Islamic and Pan Asiatic movements. In treating of the colonial situation Lenin insisted that the Communists should support the bourgeois democratic revolutionary movements for tactical reasons. By this he meant that if the Communist Party in a colonial country supported a bourgeois national leader and helped him to overthrow the colonial power, they would thereby earn a respectable place in the political life of the democracy which would be established and could then work for the overthrow of that democracy from within.

Some of the delegates, however, maintained that the Communists should never unite with a movement of this kind but should attack it and destroy it. This position was defended by the delegate from India, M. N. Roy, who was still alive and active in the Communist Party of India as late as 1963. Interestingly enough, we now find two factions in the Communist Party of India: one favoring the policy proposed by Lenin and now followed by the CPSU (the Communist Party of the Soviet Union) and the other proposed by Roy and now followed by the Communist Party of China.

Roy also rejected the view of the majority of delegates that the revolution must be completed in Europe before it could be launched in Asia. He felt that the International should foster revolution in Asia simultaneously with that of Europe. Lenin's views on these points, however, prevailed.

In an attempt to keep control of the revolutionary movements in Asia, the Comintern did call a Congress of the Peoples of the East. There were present at Baku in southern Russia workers and peasants and, of course, intellectuals and professional revolutionaries from Persia, Armenia and Turkey. It met on Sept. 1, 1920 with 1891 delegates from 32 so-called nations of the East. Nearly two thirds of these delegates were said to be Communists. However, nothing very much was accomplished though some of these leaders were given new ideas and some were brought closer to the Russians. Perhaps the main reason for the lack of success was that the Russians could not afford to sponsor revolutions at that time since they were in the midst of a serious economic crisis at home and were anxious to build up their trade with capitalist countries. Contrary to the expectations of the Second World Congress of the Comintern the Bolsheviks suffered one defeat after another both within Russia and also in Poland, Italy and Germany.

The Third World Congress of the Comintern was held in June and July, 1921 in Moscow. While world revolution was still its ultimate aim, the Congress declared that the Communist Parties of the world must support the Communist Party of the Soviet Union. The dictatorship of the proletariat in Russia must be maintained, for through it, the proletariat of the neighboring countries will eventually gain power. This Congress, then, was a definite step forward in the complete subordination of the world revolutionary movement to the needs of the Russian Communist Party. The Third World Congress of the Comintern clearly understood that the Russians were incapable of any further successful revolutionary movements at that time; that they had serious internal problems and that there was little possibility of the Communist Parties of the West achieving power within the foreseeable future.

The Sections of the Congress, where the various national Communist Parties were represented, were ordered to concern themselves with the masses of their own countries and, since they would receive little attention if they preached outright Communism, it was agreed that they should follow what eventually became known as the policy of the United Front. Actually this decision was made in December, 1921, not by a Comintern Congress but by the Executive Committee of the Comintern, a body in which the Russians had much more influence than they had in the Congress. The basic reason for such influence was that the members of the Executive Committee resided in Moscow whereas the delegates to a World Congress came from many different countries and stayed in the Soviet Union for only a short period.

There was serious opposition to the adoption of this United Front policy especially in the ranks of the French and the Italian Communist Parties. This resulted in the growth of a left and right wing within the Parties; the same important division exists today especially in the Italian Party.

In the Fourth World Congress in November and December, 1922, it was evident that Russia, as yet, had not gained complete control of the Comintern since there was opposition expressed against the United Front policy by at least four important delegates. In the final vote on the matter there were 16 abstentions and one dissenting vote, something which would not occur in the later meetings of the Comintern. However, the influence of the Russians was greater than in the previous Congress and the different national Communist Parties were instructed to give complete support to the Soviet Union. The Comintern had now become a docile tool of the CPSU and an integral part of the foreign policy of Russia.

The Comintern was seriously shaken by the events of the next year, 1923, in Germany. There a split in the Communist Party resulted in a left and a right faction. The Comintern favored the right or conservative wing of the German Communist Party. Actually a revolutionary situation existed but the Party was not capable of utilizing it. Many of the members were confused by the previous United Front tactics and decisions were made to start the revolution in the wrong areas so that all these efforts ended in complete failure.

One of the results of the failure of the revolution in Germany was to weaken the position of Zinoviev in the Comintern since he had supported the right wing faction of the German Party. Furthermore it now became clear to the Soviet Politburo that it was no longer possible for the revolution to spread through Western Europe via Germany—an idea and a hope that they had long cherished.

The Fifth World Congress met in June and July, 1924. Having complete control of the organization, the Russians were able to impose their ideas on the national sections of the Comintern. Emphasis was placed on the principle of "democratic centralism" according to which complete agreement was demanded from all the subordinate Parties. Members who disagreed could be expelled. The practical result of this principle was that the principal Communist leaders of the various countries had to agree with Russian policy or be expelled from their own Parties. The national leaders who were approved by the Russians, then, applied the principle of democratic centralism in their own parties and thus maintained unanimous support for Russian policies.

It was at this Fifth Congress that the delegates were unanimous in condemning Trotskyism in spite of the fact that Trotsky had many friends in the Comintern.

This Congress also faced the problem of the German Communist Party which was the strongest Party at that time after the Russian. Some of the Comintern leaders disagreed with Manuilski's policies regarding Germany even though he occupied a key position in the organization and was very close to Stalin. Eventually, by decision of Stalin, the so-called left group was expelled from the German Party and his loyal supporters who were the more conservative group took over the positions of power.

The main policy that the Comintern was to follow was clearly stated by Stalin at the Fourteenth Congress of the Russian Communist Party in December, 1925, when he demanded that the relationship between the Soviet Union and the proletariat of Western countries be completely changed. These proletariats, said Stalin, have a moral obligation of defending "our State against capitalism" and "our interests against imperialism."

After these failures in Europe the Comintern tried to gain influence in China. It followed the tactics of a United Front and cooperated with the Kuomintang. In the autumn of 1923 Chiang Kai-shek went to Moscow for a few months; he returned home with a number of Russian officers and Borodin, a Comintern representative. With Borodin were a number of Communists who were to become famous in later years: Roy of India, Ho Chi Minh of North Vietnam and Earl Browder of the U.S.A.

At first the United Front worked well. In fact, before his death in 1925, Sun Yat-sen described the collaboration between the Kuomintang and the Communists as the foundation of the liberation of China. However, when Chiang Kai-shek came to power the situation quickly changed. Even while he was in Moscow, Chiang seems to have realized that the Russians were planning to use him for their own purposes. In March, 1926, he imprisoned some of the Chinese Communists and also some of the Russian advisors and, as soon as the fighting ceased, he expelled the Communists from the Government. Thus the policy of the Comintern in China ended in complete failure.

The Sixth World Congress of the Comintern took place from July to September, 1928. It was clear from the beginning that its sessions were under the complete control of Stalin. He had prevented a World Congress from being called between 1925 and 1928 because he feared opposition to some of his policies especially from leftwing groups in the World Communist movement. So again we have the situation where there was an opposition faction within the Comintern but which was completely outmaneuvered by Stalin. When we refer to different groups within the Communist movement, we mean that their differences were chiefly concerned with strategy and tactics. Both groups were genuine Communists. It is in this sense that we allude to the rightwing and the leftwing of the movement.

The guiding power of the Comintern between World Congresses was the Presidium that was elected by the Executive Committee. Stalin's power was complete here in 1929 when Bukharin was removed from its leading position. Interestingly enough there was no election of a new president by the Executive Committee but Manuilski and Dimitroff together with Otto Kuusinen exercised authority in the place of Stalin. (This is the same Kuusinen who in 1959 was chairman of the committee that edited the new ideological textbook for World Communism: *The Foundations of Marxism-Leninism.*)

With the coming of the great depression in 1930, the Executive Committee thought that the situation was ripe for world revolution, particularly in Western Europe as well as China and India. Consequently the Comintern swung towards the left even though previously a number of leaders in different parts of the world had been expelled from it for belonging to the leftwing factions. But once more the Comintern was to suffer serious setbacks. Thus, for example, even though in the last free election in Germany in November, 1932, the Communist Party received nearly 6,000,000 votes, still they were not able to accomplish very much.

It was after the failure of its leftwing policies to bring about any successful revolutions during the years of the worldwide depression that the Comintern in 1934 adopted the tactics of the United Front. There was a difference of opinion in the Executive Committee as to the correctness of this policy but Stalin decided in favor of it and in this he was supported by Mao Tse-tung and by M. Thorez of the French Communist Party. Of course, as events were soon to reveal, the Popular Front was merely a means of aiding Russian foreign policy and not a sincere attempt to work together with other groups. In fact, it has been suggested that the principal reason why Stalin was interested in it was to put pressure on Hitler through France and thus bring about an agreement between Germany and Russia.

The Seventh World Congress met in July-August, 1935. There had been an interval of nearly seven years since the previous Congress was convened. Again the Congress reflected the policies of Stalin. It gave strong support to the Popular Front tactics. Though it stressed the eventual world revolution through which power would be seized in all countries, it recognized as its first duty the defense of the Soviet Union.

Here we may call attention to one of the most effective means of carrying on the Popular Front, namely, the organization of large international groups, most of whose members were not Communists but whose operating committee was usually controlled by the Party. There was, for example, the Red Trade-Union International, the Communist Youth International, the International of Communist Women and the International Red Relief. There was also the Red Teachers' International, the International League Against War and Fascism, etc. This tactic is being used at the present time especially through the World Peace Council.

After the Seventh World Congress there was an even greater development within Russia. The Executive Committee of the International came more and more under the control of the State Security Services. Then the work of the Comintern came to an end when Stalin signed the pact with Hitler on August 23, 1939. Its formal dissolution was published on the 22nd of May, 1943. This was done in order to get more military assistance for the Soviet Union from the Allies. Actually the real power over International Communism was still in the Kremlin.

In the period after the dissolution of the Comintern and before the Cominform was organized, control was exercised over the national Communist Parties by the Central Committee of the CPSU. It was the Department of International Relations which actually carried out the job. It is the opinion of Nollau that Zhadanov who signed the decision dissolving the Comintern was the Secretary within the Central Committee responsible for this department. It may be only a coincidence but he also delivered the principal speech on the occasion of the founding of the Cominform.

As for the beginnings of the Cominform, it seems that in June, 1946, when Tito was in Moscow, Stalin asked him if he thought an International should be established for the purpose of exchanging information between the Communist Parties. Nothing resulted from this discussion but a year later the Polish Communist Party invited the Communist Parties of Yugoslavia, Bulgaria, Albania, Hungary, Czechoslovakia, Italy and France as well as the Communist Party of the Soviet Union to attend a meeting which was held in September, 1947. The importance of this meeting can be seen from the names of the delegates: Malenkov, Kardelj and Djilas of Yugoslavia, Pauker and Cheorghiu-Dej of Rumania, Duclos of France, Gomulka of Poland, Slansky of Czechoslovakia and Longo of Italy. Zhadanov's speech shows that the real purpose of the Cominform was to revitalize and control leftwing policies within the European Communist Parties and thereby assist Russia in carrying out its foreign policy.

As a result of this meeting an Information Bureau was set up consisting of the representatives of the Communist

Parties present although nothing was said about a representative from the CPSU. This Bureau, then, was to serve as a means of communication between the various Communist Parties and in this way to bring about a greater coordination between the ruling Communist Parties in Eastern Europe and the leading Western European Communist Parties in the struggle against the Marshal Plan. Actually it gave the Soviet Union another means of controlling the foreign Communist Parties who were members of it.

Finally one of the tasks of this organization was to publish in a large number of languages a magazine that would carry the latest information on the Party Line for all the different Communist Parties. Meanwhile, however, the actual control of the leadership of many of these Communist Parties actually remained in the hands of the Executive Committee of the CPSU.

About a month after this meeting, the first issue of this publication appeared. Stalin had given it the name, *For Lasting Peace, For People's Democracy*. It was edited in Belgrade by Pavel Yudin, a Russian who brought several compositors with him from Moscow and who immediately established radiotelephone and teleprinter communications with Moscow. Nollau says that security precautions were so strict that, during workbreaks and at night Yudin's assistant locked up the rooms and sealed the doors where the paper was being printed. Nor was this enough for the Russians. The paper had to be pre-censored in Moscow and a number of Soviet journalists were placed on the editorial staff.

In 1948 a permanent editorial staff was set up with

representatives from the different countries. There were between forty and fifty people on this staff and despite the fact that nearly thirty of these were in the Russian department the policy of pre-censorship in Moscow was continued. The paper thus was a clear guide to the Communist Parties of the world as to the policy of the CPSU.

At the end of March, 1948, Stalin and Molotov began using the Cominform as a means of dominating Yugoslavia. They first sent a letter not to Yugoslavia alone but to all the members of the Cominform in which they complained that Yugoslav Communists were criticizing the CPSU. The Yugoslavs, in turn, sent an answer to all the other Parties but the replies of these Parties came to Belgrade not directly but by way of the Central Committee of the CPSU and the Soviet representative in Belgrade.

Tito realized that the other Parties would follow the CPSU and he therefore refused to bring the points under debate before the Cominform. However, a meeting took place in Bucharest in June, 1948, which resulted in the expulsion of the Yugoslav Party from the Cominform and the transfer of the headquarters of the organization from Belgrade to Bucharest. The CPSU rightly viewed Tito's show of independence as a very serious development, especially since the primary purpose of the establishment of the Cominform was to maintain Russian domination over the Parties that belonged to the Cominform. However, it is worthwhile noting that at the 5th Congress of the Yugoslav Party in July, 1948, when the delegates were considering the relation of Tito with the Soviet Union, Tito did not attack the CPSU nor did he deny any Communist principles. He simply said that he had a difference of opinions on some tactics with some of the leaders of that important Communist Party.

The campaign against Tito then became a pretext for crushing any show of national independence within the various Parties. The general line was expressed in one of the papers of the German Communist Party where it was said that the only true internationalist is one who fights with all his might against the enemies of the Soviet Union. In Albania, Bulgaria, Hungary, Czechoslovakia and East Germany a number of important Communist leaders were imprisoned and executed. In Poland, among those jailed was the present leader, W. Gomulka. The terror was halted only by the death of Stalin. Khrushchev, in order to improve relations with Tito agreed to the dissolution of the Cominform and on April 17, 1956 the announcement was made in the Cominform newspaper. By this time, the leaders of many of the Communist Parties (especially those in whose country there were no Soviet divisions) understood that it was now possible to be more or less independent of Moscow. And this was especially true after the leadership of the CPSU had gone to Belgrade in 1955 and, in effect, had apologized to Tito.

But it was at the 20th Party Congress of the CPSU that the basis was laid for a further breakdown in the control exercised by the CPSU over the other national Communist Parties. There was some acceptance of the idea of individual roads to Socialism. There was open admission of many mistakes and even crimes on the part of Stalin. Communism in 1956, it was indicated, was to be different. Then, in the same year, there were the uprisings in Poland and in Hungary. The national Communist Parties of these countries wanted to be independent of Moscow. As we noted above, it was between the 20th Party Congress of the CPSU and the uprisings that the official notice of the dissolution of the Cominform was published in April, 1956. The iron discipline which Stalin had exercised over foreign Communist Parties through the Comintern was now gone —perhaps forever.

Though the individual parties wanted to be independent, they still desired to cooperate with the other Communist Parties. Togliatti, the Italian Communist leader, referred to this new situation in 1956 as "polycentralism" in the Communist Movement. A distinction was made in the relations of the CPSU and Communist Parties which controlled their governments by reason of their country having been liberated by the Soviet forces; Communist Parties that ruled in countries where they had gained power without Soviet forces actually turning over this power to them; and countries where Communist Parties were not in power. "In this situation," said Togliatti, "relations with the CPSU and the great Soviet Communist movement appear in a new light."

A number of the Communist Parties of Western Europe agreed with Togliatti's criticism of the CPSU but they still looked to Moscow for guidance. The official "line" appeared in an article that was printed by Pravda, the official paper of the CPSU on June 27, 1956. Written by Eugene Dennis, then General Secretary of the CPUSA, it confirmed the admissibility of individual roads to Socialism and urged the adoption of a new Popular Front policy that called for the cooperation with "progressive" groups. This general statement was followed a few days later, June 30,

1956, by a resolution of the Central Committee of the CPSU. This admitted that there had been mistakes made in the past but ascribed them to Stalin rather than to the Soviet system. No reference was made to Togliatti's "polycentralism" nor the question of individual roads to socialism. There was simply a call for ideological unity and international fraternal solidarity. There was not even a clear reference to the "leading role of the Soviet Union."

A comparison of the situation of the Communist Party of Poland in Stalin's time with its role in 1956 gives us a vivid picture of the radical change in the power relationships of the CPSU and some of the Communist Parties. According to Armstrong, the Polish Communist leaders were summoned to a meeting in 1938 in Moscow. There they were brought before a commission composed of Manuilski, Dimitroff and Kuusinen who accused them of treason and espionage. Nearly all of them were executed or died in concentration camps. Lowenthal points out that of the top Yugoslav party leaders in Moscow, Tito alone seems to have gotten out alive—and with power to reorganize the Yugoslav Party. He must have been considered the most loyal Stalinist. In August of 1956, however, Gomulka who had been expelled from the Party through the Russians' influence and who only recently was released from prison, was readmitted to the Party. On October 16, 1956, it was announced that he had attended the meeting of the Polish Politburo and three days later, while a Russian plane, carrying Khrushchev, Kaganovitch, Mikoyan and Molotov was circling over Warsaw waiting for permission to land, he was voted into the Central Committee of the Polish Party. The Russians apparently soon discovered that they could not impose their will because they left the next day without having achieved anything. In fact the following day, October 21, Gomulka was elected First Secretary of the Polish Party. Nevertheless the Russians understood that the Polish Party was not anti-Russian and that it was a true Communist Party. They recognized Gomulka as a true Communist but not completely under their control.

The fact that the CPSU desired to maintain the same control over the Communist Parties of Central Europe that Stalin had exercised became clear from the events in Hungary. Tito reports that in his visit to Moscow in June, 1956, there was a discussion about the leadership of the Communist Party in Hungary and the Soviet leaders spoke of the Hungarian Party in such a way as to indicate that they had control of it. Moreover, Mikoyan took part in a meeting of the Central Committee of the Hungarian Communist Party on July 18, 1956, during which Rakosi was relieved of the leadership.

Then Russia intervened militarily in Hungary on the 24th of October, 1956, and yet, on the 30th of October, the Soviet Government declared its respect for the principle of complete equality between Socialist States, which involved the duty of non-interference in the internal affairs of other Socialist States, respect for their territorial integrity and national sovereignty. On November 1, 1956, when the Soviet forces were preparing to reenter Budapest, Mikoyan and Suslov entered negotiations for the withdrawal of the Russian troops with the Prime Minister Imre Nagy, who was assisted by Munnich and Janos Kadar, then First Secretary of the Party. It is now known that on the evening of that same day Munnich (who was Minister of Interior in the Hungarian Government and a veteran of the Spanish Civil War) and Kadar visited the Soviet Embassy. How successfully they carried on their treason is seen from the fact that even three days later on November 4 the Hungarian Government still did not have any doubts about the loyalty of these two.

It is clear, then, that it was through this means, that is, the help of local leaders who were completely subordinated to the CPSU, together with the use of the Red Army, that Communist control was imposed upon Hungary.

The intervention of the Red Army, however, was to create a severe crisis for the Communist Parties in many countries. Some of the Parties, such as the American, Danish and Norwegian, condemned the Soviet action (this eventually led to a change in their leadership). Others such as the French, Czech, East German and Italian gave full support to the Russian action. (This was not surprising when we recall that these leaders had been able to remain in power so long only because of the support they received from the CPSU.) The Polish Party, however, allowed public criticism of Khrushchev's Hungarian policy and in this they were supported by the Chinese and Chou En-lai. We have, therefore, the interesting situation where many Communists spoke of Khrushchev's policy as "Stalinist" and the Chinese Communists were against it.

Actually, from these events it was clear that, even though the Soviet Union talked of non-intervention in the affairs of other Socialist countries, it reserved the right to intervene whenever there was danger that the Communist Government would be overthrown.

Before the end of the 1950's, many of the world's Communist Parties passed resolutions acknowledging the fact that the Soviet Union stood at the center of proletarian internationalism. However, more recently, the Polish, Yugoslav and Chinese Communist Parties have failed to make use of these phrases. They limit themselves to speaking of the CPSU as the original, leading Communist Party of the world, the Party that carried out the great October revolution, etc. But they refuse to recognize the CPSU as having the dominant role in international communism. Further, it is noticeable that in the declaration published in November, 1957, by the representatives of the Communist and Workers Parties of the Socialist countries no particular tribute was paid to the CPSU. It was simply stated that peace was being defended by the Socialist countries with the Soviet Union as their leader. Thus the present situation seems to be that the Communist Parties of different countries, depending upon how much their Communist leaders obtained their positions through their own efforts and independently of the CPSU, strive to be independent in the internal affairs of their countries and to gain a more equitable arrangement in their economic relations with the Soviet Union. On the other hand, the CPSU has done everything possible to maintain its power in the Communist parties of Eastern Europe through its own agents, its military forces and its economic ties.

There has been a desire expressed by some of the national Communist leaders, who are dependent on the Soviet Union, to set up some sort of a central organization where opinions could be exchanged and ideas and policies formulated but the Polish, Italian and Yugoslav parties were against any such organization. The fact is that, since Moscow was no longer able to dominate completely an international Communist organization, the existence of such organizations sometimes created problems for the CPSU. Thus at the November, 1956 meeting of the World Peace Council, one of the most important Communist international front organizations, there was a great deal of criticism of the Soviet invasion of Hungary. The same problem arose in regard to the Communist controlled International Association of Democratic Lawyers. The CPSU must have decided in late 1956 that, instead of setting up a new Cominform, the better policy would be to keep direct contact with the individual Communist Parties and to have personal contacts with the Party leaders.

In November, 1957, the Fortieth Anniversary of the October Revolution was celebrated in Moscow. All of the Parties that attended agreed to a very mild Peace Manifesto but the more important Declaration by representatives of the Communist and Workers Parties of the Socialist Countries was signed only by the representatives of the 12 Communist Parties that were governing various countries. This resolution called for a growth of unity and solidarity in the world movement and implied a recognition of the dominance of the CPSU. Interestingly enough Mao Tse-tung was one of the leaders who did sign the Declaration. Yugoslavia, of course, did not sign and even though the Polish Communist Party did, nearly a year later in Warsaw Gomulka made the statement that there was no longer an international center for the Communist movement nor was there any need to create one.

Nollau summarizes the results of the Moscow Declaration regarding international collaboration between the Communist Parties as follows: No new International was founded; bi-lateral and multi-lateral discussions will be held between the CPSU and the national CPs in which current problems will be discussed and experiences exchanged; the internal affairs of a Party must not be decided during discussions with other Parties and the agenda for such discussions must be made known to all participants beforehand; and there should be published an international Marxist-Leninist periodical (we now have it in English under the title of *The World Marxist Review*).

After the refusal of the Yugoslavs to sign the Moscow Declaration of 1957, the CPSU realized that they were not going to be able to gain control of that party again. Then in order to weaken the Yugoslav leadership and nullify the effects of their independent action, the Russians carried on a strong campaign against them through propaganda and diplomatic means.

Another source of disunity for international communism in recent years has been the leadership of the Chinese Communist Party. After the uprising in the Eastern European satellites in 1956, the Chinese, for the first time, took an active part in the affairs of that area. Though they supported the idea of individual roads to socialism, nevertheless they called on the satellites to recognize the leadership of the Soviet Union. This was done probably because the Chinese themselves were dependent on the military power of the Russians and were afraid that, if more trouble developed in Eastern Europe, Russia would have to concentrate its power there.

The Chinese certainly did not look upon the Russian leaders as capable of giving good advice to other national

Communists. For they had received their share of bad advice from the Kremlin. In the 1920's Stalin advised them to work with the Kuomintang and when they did so they ultimately suffered a severe defeat from which they did not recover for many years. In fact, Mao Tse-tung (the first and for many years the only Party leader who became such without orders from Moscow) achieved his first great success by following a strategy not approved by Moscow. And, at the end of the Second World War, though Stalin urged Mao to join a coalition government, he refused and carried on his revolution with the result that he gained control of all of mainland China.

The Chinese wanted to assert their independence of and equality with the Soviets. They had to move cautiously, however, since they were still in need of economic aid from Russia. (Later Chou En-lai was to thank the Soviets for the 10,000 technicians they sent to China during the first ten years that country was controlled by the Communists.)

An attempt to settle the differences between Moscow and Peiping was made at the time of the issuance of the Moscow Declaration in 1957 but with little success. Among the many reasons for the conflict were the following: the failure of the Soviets to support an invasion of Taiwan, the hasty introduction of the communes into China, the gradual reduction of economic and technical assistance from the Soviets to the Chinese and the difference in opinion between Russia and China over the latter's policies in reference to Tibet and India together with an intense dislike of Khrushchev's visit to the U.S. with its emphasis on peaceful coexistence in 1959.

There were lengthly discussions of the differences between the CPSU and the CPC during November and December, 1960, when the representatives of 81 Communist Parties met in Moscow but no solution acceptable to both sides was reached. The Chinese and their allies remained so belligerent that Khrushchev had to discuss the matter publicly and at length during the 22nd Congress of the CPSU which was held in Moscow in October, 1961. Finally during the Spring and Summer of 1963 both sides published lengthy charges and replies.

Now what is the relationship between the various Communist parties? On one side we have the Yugoslavs who now are friendly to the Russians though independent of them; then we have the Chinese on the other side. They consider the Yugoslavs as traitors to the revolution. Between them we have the Russians who are still the strongest Communist group both militarily and economically. However the Chinese compete with the Russians for influence in the nations of Asia and Africa and, to a lesser degree, even in Latin America. Some Parties have aligned themselves with the Chinese: the Albanians, the North Koreans, the Indonesians, the Japanese, the Malayans, the Siamese, one of the Burmese Parties, together with important Party groups in India, Brazil, Cuba, Belgium, Italy, etc.

Next we have the Communist Party of Poland. Its leader, Gomulka, was imprisoned during Stalin's reign and he gained power despite the opposition of Khrushchev. While cooperating with the CPSU, he maintains a position between the Yugoslavs and the Russians. (The other Eastern European Parties are moving in the same direction.)

Moreover, we have serious dissensions in many of the other Communist Parties. In most cases, it is true, these have been solved by the expulsion of those leaders who protested against too much subservience to Moscow. This occurred in the CPUSA, the Canadian Labor Progressive Party, the Danish Party, the Dutch Party and others.

It must be said, therefore, that Moscow has had no success in its efforts to regain a position of strict control over the international Communist movement such as it enjoyed under Stalin. At the present time, the Russians are forced to use other means for bringing pressure to bear on many of the Parties. They station large diplomatic staffs in countries, they send delegates from their Central Committee to the Central Committee of the Party in another country; they hold International Meetings, they invite prominent Communists to the Soviet Union for vacations, for health treatments or to be observers at the Party Congress of the CPSU; they still have a large number of young Communist leaders who attend the Party schools in the Soviet Union, and so form close links between the future leadership in these countries and the CPSU; some of the members like Kuusinen devote considerable time to cultivating foreign Communist leaders; others, like Suslov, attend the Party Congresses in various countries and make known their opinions in these meetings. Moreover, there is an active department of international relations in the Central Committee of the CPSU, run by Yurii Antropov who was Soviet Ambassador in Hungary at the time of the Revolution in 1956.

There is also the international journal known in the United States as *The World Marxist Review* (Problems of Peace and Socialism). Its editor is Alexey Rumyantsev who was formerly editor of the *Kommunist,* the theoretical journal of the Central Committee of the CPSU. Representatives from the editorial staff of this magazine attend regional international Communist meetings and offer "guidance" to those present. The purpose of the magazine, of course, is to let the foreign parties know the Moscow line. It also encourages meetings such as that held in August, 1959, when Communist theoreticians and historians from twenty-five countries met in Bucharest for a discussion of the problem of revisionism in the Communist movement. An editorial Council was set up in Prague where the paper is edited and Communists from 36 countries attended a meeting in April, 1960.

The editorial staff of this paper has a section known as the Department of the National Liberation Movement which deals with Communist Party activities in colonial and former colonial areas. This and other facts indicate that the staff of the paper does not limit itself merely to publishing.

To summarize, we may say that a study of the international aspect of Communism reveals the following stages. At first, there were independent Communist groups that held international conferences. Next the First International was organized. Its directing committee was truly international and its national Parties were equal. It did, however, eventually expel Bukarhin, the anarchist, for being too radical.

The Second International was organized 13 years after the dissolution of the First. It represented many workers' organizations but was paralyzed almost from the beginning by the Marxists and non-Marxist factions. It was less centralized than the First International and was a very weak organization. For all purposes it died during the First World War.

The Third International was organized under Lenin's influence. The Parties who belonged were supposed to be equal. Theoretically, the Russian CP was only one section of the Comintern. A number of the Parties maintained their independence for some years but gradually under Stalin all the parties came under the complete control of the CPSU. After the Second World War, however, the Parties in Yugoslavia and in China were no longer under the control of the Soviets. Then, following the death of Stalin, the Polish Party asserted a noticeable independence and there was talk of "polycentralism" within International Communism. Finally, we had the differences between Russia and China; those are now a matter of public record. Other means are now being utilized to gain the "voluntary" cooperation of many of the national Communist Parties with the CPSU.

Nevertheless, though there are serious differences in the international movement and we no longer have a monolithic organization such as we had in the late 1930's, all of the Parties are Communists and are actually supporting some common policies voluntarily despite their differences in other matters.

A New Method of Bringing the Redemption and Morality to People

▶▶

JAMES KERINS, C.SS.R., Ph.D.

> For we preach not ourselves,
>   But Christ Jesus as Lord,
>   And ourselves merely as your servants
>   in Christ Jesus.
> For God, who commanded light
>   to shine out of darkness,
>   has shone in our hearts, to give
>   enilghtenment concerning the
>   knowledge of the glory of God,
>   shining on the Face of Christ Jesus.
> But we carry this treasure
>   in vessels of clay,
>   to show that the abundance of the power
>   is God's, and not ours.
>
> (2 Corinthians, 4)

The final command Christ gave to His apostles before His ascension was "Go, teach all nations. . . ." That the apostles and their successors heeded that instruction is attested to by the phenomenal momentum of the early expansion of the Church. Over the centuries, her missionaries have penetrated to the farthest corners of the earth, carrying the Gospel with them. Yet, their sincerity and self-sacrifice has not always guaranteed success in their mission—chiefly, it would appear, because of misconceptions as to the effective methods to be employed, and because of too close an association between the essence of the Christian message and the externals of Western culture.

Today, the Church is increasingly alert to the importance of approach and method in preaching the word of God. She has recognized the necessity of adapting means to milieu. . . . Father Mateo Ricci's Chinese venture would doubtless find stronger support today, when Congo rhythms punctuate the Mass in Africa, when Benedictine monks have founded their monasteries in Asia and Africa where "Ora et labora" is already an accepted concept. A fresh look at the ancient Eastern rites of the Church has revealed their attractiveness to many peoples repelled by the Latin rite for various reasons, mainly, perhaps, its association with Western civilization in some of the latter's least edifying manifestations.

In line with this consideration of effective missionary effort is that of the means whereby the non-Catholic in our own society—the man who distrusts the "Roman" of Roman Catholic, who hesitates to enter a church or rectory—may be attracted into making contact with the Church. One solution to this problem has been the establishment of the "information center," an easily accessible, non-parochial, informal enironment offering a variety of services. Ideally, it is equipped to present Catholic teaching in a comfortable atmosphere, in the sense that the inquirer may feel no need to commit himself, may even remain anonymous if he pleases, until he has looked the situation over. In our American society, this approach seems to enjoy some success. Over fifty information centers are now open in the United States; they offer a diversity of facilities: instruction, library, information by telephone and mail, counseling, etc.

In 1956, the Redemptorist Fathers were invited by Archbishop Patrick O'Boyle of Washington to organize and staff an information center for the archdiocese. For Redemptorists, it was a new task, but one clearly in line with there calling to "help those who are most in need of the assistance of the Church." (The frenetic pace of modern living cannot conceal the reality . . . surely the souls whose need of the Church's help is greatest are to be found here, in the technologically advanced society of our age, a society in which a man walks in fear of losing not just his life, but his very identity as a human being.)

The staff chosen for the center, Father James Kerins and Father James Coen, made a survey of centers already in existence, and found a bewildering variety of opinions on the essential functions to be fulfilled. One or two points were obvious: a midtown location and a program of instruction classes were basic requirements. Should there be a library? A chapel? Masses? What about selling religious articles, as in San Francisco? Or scheduling lectures by visiting speakers, as in Boston and Toronto?

The decision on most of these questions must depend finally on the available financial support and the size of the staff. For the Washington center, a limited budget restricted the size of the premises and the number of persons to be hired—one receptionist. More ambitious projects, such as lecture programs by eminent speakers who appreciate an emolument, would have to be bypassed. Competing with already well-established religious goods stores was undesirable as well as physically impossible. The size of the professional staff, two priests, made it necessary to plan carefully for the most efficient and productive schedule possible. The first year was one of some experimentation in programming. The Fathers began their day at 10:30 A.M. and ended it around 9:00 P.M., with classes in the evening hours four days a week.

The problem of location was solved happily; though not overlarge, the offices are ideally situated in the business and banking district, close to transportation from all parts of the Washington and Northern Virginia areas. (The center is also about two blocks from the White House—in the eyes of some visitors it basks in its reflected glow, in the eyes of others, it lurks in its shadows—it all depends on the political point of view!) A chapel seating thirty-three, a classroom, a library and reception area, and a small office for each of the priests occupy all of the space available. This took about a year to complete, although the center was open and active during most of that period. The former Washington Catholic Library was taken over, and has since been considerably expanded by purchases of current books.

Once the physical and financial boundaries were established, a policy of unlimited service was adopted. Rather than confine itself strictly to convert instruction—its primary function, to be sure—the center would attempt to handle any and every need that arose, in so far as it was capable. The needs made themselves felt very soon: marital, spiritual, moral problems galore, and questions, questions, questions, by mail, by phone, in person. At the same time, every effort was made to establish cordial and co-operative relations with the local parishes. By its very nature, an information center may find itself occupying an anomalous position in the diocese unless its staff takes care to define its functions and limitations firmly and then adhere to that definition. It may be said here that the Washington center enjoys excellent relations with both chancery and rectory circles.

Perhaps a few specific details on the aspects of the work in the Washington information center will serve as an indication of the problems encountered in the field in general. Though small, the center seems to combine in its narrow physical limits almost all of the facets of information center activity. The primary one is, of course, the convert apostolate.

In our approach to recruiting interested persons for instruction, we have followed the tried and true formula: newspaper advertisements before each series of classes begins (No cost! No obligation!); mailed schedules, throw-aways, and—surest of all methods—word of mouth invitation from born Catholics and converts who know the center. The lectures are programmed in sets of two series, each set running from thirteen to fifteen weeks at the rate of two hours a week. The first series is given on Mondays and Wednesdays at 5:30 P.M., the second on Tuesdays and Thursdays at 7:00 P.M. The first set begins in January and ends before Easter, the second starts after Easter and ends early in August. After a period of vacation in August, the last set of lectures begins in September and ends before Christmas.

Inevitably, non-Catholics comprise only part of the attendance; Catholic partners in mixed marriages, Catholic fiances, CCD students looking for pointers, laity taking a refresher course in the doctrine of their faith, all are likely to be found in the classes in the course of a year.

Employing the Christ-centered approach, and making use of such visual aids as films, filmstrips, and blackboard, the Fathers themselves give the hour-long lectures. Their work is greatly facilitated by the assistance of the Legion of Mary. The Praesidium of Mary, Co-Redemptrix was established at the center for the specific purpose of helping with the inquiry classes. The members have attended at least one complete course of the lectures and have received additional training from the Fathers. Their method, outlined in a handbook expressly prepared for this group, has been instrumental in establishing the atmosphere of warmth and cordiality indispensable to the success of a convert class. Legion members are prepared to answer questions before and after the lecture, demonstrate and explain Catholic practices, teach the common Catholic prayers and the Rosary, distribute literature, and serve coffee. The lectures are always presented extemporaneously—or as extemporaneously as can be after six years of talking on the same subjects—and each member of the class is provided with a copy of Kilgallon and Weber's *Life in Christ* as supplementary reading. In addition, a pamphlet on the subject of the current lecture is distributed to encourage further study and questions.

As the series proceeds, the Legion members ascertain by discreet inquiry the religion of those in the class, and their intentions, if any, regarding baptism. Private appoint-

ments are arranged with the priest for those who wish
to be baptized, or who have some personal matter to discuss with him. The end of the course usually brings several new converts for baptism. During recent years, the
Fathers have baptized their converts at the Cathedral of
St. Matthew, where the record is entered. The center keeps
a record of instructions and baptisms, and enters the name
of the new Catholic on the mailing list for schedules and
the *St. Paul Guild Bulletin,* a follow-up paper sent out to
converts. The center now publishes this bulletin, having
taken over the operation from an assistant at St. Matthew's.

While a large number of converts are the fruit of the
inquiry classes, an even greater number are baptized after
private instruction. These persons may be unable or unwilling to attend the class. Some people prefer the privacy
of individual instruction, others the "anonymity" of the
class. Probably individual instruction is the ideal, for it
proceeds at a more leisurely pace, with time for questions
and discussion, and—most important of all—a beginning
can be made in spiritual formation. A habit of prayer is
more thoroughly inculcated, and the priest is better able
to judge the capacity of his prospective convert for a
meaningful relationship with God.

It might be noted here that one extremely difficult problem that arises in connection with the convert apostolate
is the link with marriage cases. So many people ask to take
instructions in order to "straighten out" the invalid marriage or obtain a privilege of faith. It is in this area that the
well-meaning assurances of "Catholic friends"—who are
presumably not too well versed in divine or ecclesiastical
law—constitute a veritable hazard. Armed with this advice,

the would-be convert presents himself for instruction as a sort of necessary evil to be undergone before he can marry the girl. The moral implications of cases in which the Catholic party has allowed the situation to develop to the point where the previously married non-Catholic must face this crisis will not be discussed here; suffice it to say that the extremely low number of favorable replies in privilege of faith cases is indicative of the frustrating nature of this aspect of the apostolate—not least from the point of view of the priest. Each case has its own peculiar difficulties, requires an enormous amount of paper work and ill-afforded time, and poses a serious problem in judgment as to the applicant's sincerity. Another difficulty is posed by the divergence of attitudes of the chanceries, several of which are unwilling to accept such cases at all.

A more cheering side to the marriage-convert instruction phenomenon is presented when the non-Catholic partner in an invalid marriage comes in to take instructions with a view to having the marriage validated. The fallen-away spouse returns to the Church, thanks to the unselfish concern of the wife—for it is usually the non-Catholic wife who takes the positive step.

While largely absorbed in convert work, information centers in general have noted (and this has inspired "agonized reappraisals" on their part) that of recent years the trend of their activity has been toward counseling. Increasing numbers of Catholics have turned to the centers when faced with spiritual and moral troubles. Why? They have priests in their own parishes, yet they come to a stranger. Obviously, one reason is that they do not want their parish rectory to know. Also, in Washington, and probably in most large cities, there is a large floating population of Catholics who never register in a parish or attend their parish church. Some have been "just staying" in Washington for ten or more years!

If the center accepted all applicants for counseling, the staff would soon be swamped and would have to abandon all other work. The Fathers deal with as many problems as they can, mostly on an emergency basis, but must resort to references to the few available professional marriage counselors and psychiatrists, and to the local pastors. Nevertheless, a large portion of the calendar of appointments is occupied by interviews with Catholics who come in search of spiritual counseling, advice in marital, psychological, and family dilemmas.

The combined role of father confessor, psychologist, teacher, pastoral counselor, this is what a priest in an information center learns through hard experience in daily contact with an ever-changing clientele. Many are the times he breathes a sigh of gratitude for the moment he can snatch for a brief visit to the chapel, the one oasis of peace.

The name "Catholic Information Center" invites and receives a rather broad interpretation. It is in its secondary, or possibly tertiary, "information" activity that the center makes most of its contacts with the public. An air of bustle—indeed chaos—surrounds the reception desk, where the telephone is busy at all hours. Government officials, news agencies, parish organizations, office workers in the midst of heated discussion, callers who want a simple answer to the problem of predestination and free will, hecklers . . . anyone and everyone may be seeking information related even remotely to the Catholic Church. Most of the time of the lay receptionist-cum-librarian is taken up in answering telephone inquiries that range from the factual to the theoretical, and sometimes the fantastic.

It may be said that in many instances these questions are revelatory of the frightening ignorance of their faith in which Catholics can remain even in these days of the progressive laity. This does not mean to say merely that current affairs, or the ecumenical movement, or the latest encyclical are the subject of inquiry; too often it is fundamental moral teaching, the simplest catechism topic, that the Catholic caller needs to have explained. Another aspect revealed in these contacts is the inability or unwillingness of many Catholics to think for themselves; they want a pronouncement from the priest on many social, political, business, and community matters with which a mature person should be capable of dealing. A narrowness of intellect, mistrust of things not specifically Catholic, sometimes a completely distorted view of their own religion—often notable in those whose education has been strictly parochial —characterizes a large number of the Catholics who call.

Evidence is not lacking, however, of the wonderful effects of the CCD programs, the interest awakened by Vatican Council II, the response to the warmth and charity of the late Holy Father, the appeals to the laymen to assume a more responsible role in the life of the Church; these are all reflected in the telephone calls and in the patronage of the library. The center's library, constantly expanded with new acquisitions, provides a wealth of material for discussion club leaders, lawyers, students, businessmen, as well as the reader of ascetical and devotional literature. The Catholic visitor may purchase pamphlets on a variety of subjects, choose from a selection of paperbacks, or use the available reference works in order to broaden his religious education. The periodicals displayed and sold in the center—*America, Commonweal, Jubilee, Sign, Ave Maria, Catholic World, Catholic Digest, Marriage, Liguorian*—certainly provide instruction and comment on all aspects of Catholic life in America and on national policies and problems. Reference copies of *Critic, Worship, The Bible, Today, Social Order, Catholic Mind, The Pope Speaks, Perspectives, Cross Currents* have been introduced in hope of arousing further interest in them.

The library serves also as an auxiliary to the Fathers in their instruction and counseling, for they often recommend selected reading to supplement their lectures. For both Catholic and non-Catholic it is a source of specialized education that is as easily accessible and as inexpensive as the public library.

Almost from the beginning, the facilities of the center have been made available to various groups for meetings. The Patricians, a discussion club for Catholics, meets in the conference room once a month to consider topics such as Mariology, Scriptures, the United Nations, mental health and religion, etc. Sponsored by the Legion of Mary, the club invites all Catholics to attend and to contribute their opinions during the discussion period, when everyone present is given an opportunity to express himself. A layman and a priest lead the discussion and summarize the findings of the meeting.

On Wednesday evenings throughout the year, a group of Recovery, Inc., a mental self-help organization, meets at the center. This is the parent group in this area, and was originally sponsored by the staff of the center. Former mental patients and persons with nervous ailments who have been recommended by their doctors attend meetings supervised by a trained layman. Their vade mecum is *Mental Health Through Will Training* by Dr. Abraham Low, founder of Recovery, Inc., and with this book and tape recordings of Dr. Low's lectures as guides, they conduct a sort of group therapy. Non-sectarian in membership and non-religious in orientation, the Recovery method is regarded by many psychiatrists as a practical therapy for nervous problems.

At one time or another, the center has also provided meeting space for the Daughters of Isabella, the Catholic War Veterans' Auxiliary, college alumnae groups, and Auxiliaries of the Legion of Mary.

The heart of the Catholic Information Center in Washington is the tiny, exquisitely neat and simple chapel. There, a dialogue Mass is offered daily at noon, with the capacity congregation responding from missals furnished by the center. The dialogue Mass was begun soon after the chapel opened, and has been popular with workers in the nearby offices, many of whom attend daily. These people, and those who snatch a few minutes on their coffee break or on the way home to stop in for a visit to the Blessed Sacrament are the chief supplementary financial and moral support of the center's work, and their interest and enthusiasm have done much to expand the center's influence.

A few statistics to impress the reader: in the past six years, the telephone has been answered about 70,000 times; more than 1,000 persons have attended the classes; about 300 have been baptized into the Faith; and the two Fathers have counseled and dealt personally with some 15,000 people.

From our own experience as well as from that of other information centers, we can safely draw the conclusion that the information center is here to stay. The need has been demonstrated, and the day is not very far away when every diocese will have at least one. The news reports indicate that centers are opening not only in the United States, but also in Latin America, where the majority of the population is, at least nominally, Catholic. Merely on the basis of their utility in the sphere of public relations, diocesan sponsorship of such centers is eminently reasonable. The center must, however, be allowed to preserve the flexibility of operation that contributes so much to its usefulness. Rigid patterns of scheduling will only serve to place it in a position where it can no longer pursue its goals, as it becomes less and less accessible to the man in the street.

It is true that centers have failed, but the failures have been few, and have been due almost entirely to shortage of money or manpower. Reasonably well-planned and well-located centers have prospered. In general, the "prosperity" has not been financial. Indeed, if there is such a thing as a dedicated money-losing venture, the Washington center can walk off with the title.

Further encouragement toward the increase of the number of information centers should come from the fact that in the present-day world, where literacy and education are spreading so rapidly, religious education must progress if religion itself is to survive as a living reality. Many years ago, the Catholic Evidence Guild pioneered the approach to the common man via the soapbox; today's information centers are an up-to-date form of the old soapbox.

Who should staff an information center? Whoever can. Some are staffed by diocesan clergy, others by religious. None can function properly without the help of devoted laymen. The Washington center has been greatly assisted by volunteer evening receptionists, in addition to its paid receptionist, sacristan, and the Legion of Mary. In view of the inevitable growth of the center movement, training classes for young priests cannot be far in the future.

If religious staff a center, two problems arise, one general and the other particular.

One of the matters for discussion at the Second Vatican Council is reportedly the relations between the diocese and exempt religious. It is no secret that these relations have not always been smooth. Our experience indicates that certain practical rules can be followed: leave matters of parish jurisdiction to the parish, make certain that diocesan authorities know precisely what the center is doing, sternly refuse to be a sounding board for criticism of the parish priests, etc.; the rules are made as the situations arise.

The particular problem for a religious results from the inability to coordinate the schedule of work in the center with the regular community life . . . at least in the case of our center. The office workday requires that we leave the monastery before ten o'clock in the morning and return after nine in the evening five days a week; this obviously plays havoc with the community life. If the center is blessed, as we are, with a lovely little chapel, private devotion can provide a fairly good substitute. When the work of the apostolate makes such demands on his time, the real danger for the religious is to lose the religious spirit.

In practice, neither of these obstacles has caused insuperable difficulties to the staff of the Washington center, as we feel that after only six years, we may still be in the experimental stage! It must be admitted, however, that an arrangement such as that of the Paulist information center in Boston, where monastery and center, as well as chapel, are co-located, could well be the ideal. There, a number of priests are available for instruction, advice, and consultation; others celebrate Mass at frequent intervals through the day; and we presume that when the burden is shared by so many, it does not weigh quite so heavily. Certainly a more reasonable schedule can be maintained, and participation in community exercises at regular hours is facilitated.

To conclude: for us, the Washington Catholic Information Center has been a great adventure. Here, we have made direct contact with the people who are most in need of help, and have the satisfaction of knowing that we have expended our time, energy, prayers, and pain in a most worthy apostolate. We have learned to marvel at the quiet strength and resignation of the suffering, to sympathize with the weak and helpless, to rejoice with the sheep that has been found. We have encountered the gamut of human ills—spiritual, mental, emotional—and done our best even when we knew it was not enough. We have wept when madness and suicide took those whom we have known, in spite of all our efforts and prayers. Certainly we have found a sphere in which our priesthood is exercised to the fullest in a parish that encompasses a world. We are grateful for this opportunity, and look forward to years of endeavor and, we hope, of expansion.

The Parish Today

►►

THOMAS J. HARTE, C.SS.R., Ph.D.

It is difficult to overestimate the importance of the parish for the apostolate of the universal Church in the modern world. Development of doctrine and broad ecclesiastical policy decisions will continue to emanate immediately from Rome, and in lesser measure from the Chanceries and Universities of the Christian world, but these will be implemented and realized for the most part at the local parish level. This has always been true in the past and, because of the nature of human social organization, will continue to be true in the future.

The Church comes to grips concretely with the impact and problems of scientific, technological, political and social change through her parishes which are spread throughout the Christian world. The rising tide of nationalism in many mission areas, the spread of democratic ideals, increased industrialization and technological progress, all these in some measure directly affect the lives of hundreds of millions throughout the world. When people are involved the Church is involved and the basic issues will be joined quite generally at the parish level. The local parish, whether urban, suburban or rural, whether in well-developed or developing areas of the world, receives the first and fullest impact, spiritually and economically, of increased industrialization and urbanization, with the usual concomitants of high mobility, secularization and the breakdown of traditional social organization and traditional values.

It must be emphasized at this point that the parish is not only a very important unit in the structural and functional systems of the Church but that it also operates within and is directly affected by the local and national secular systems, whether cultural, social, economic or political, with which it interacts continually. This is an extremely important point in a period of rapid and radical social change such as our own times. Within a few years, sometimes within a few months, a given parish may undergo a radical change in the size of its population and/or in the racial, ethnic or religious composition of its people. As a result some of its traditional services and apostolic techniques become obsolete, and these must be replaced by new institutions and new pastoral approaches better adapted to the social and cultural needs of the population which it currently serves. The successful parish of today and tomorrow is one which is capable of quickly adapting itself to the needs of unstable, highly mobile, sometimes class, or race or ethnic group conscious, and often socially disorganized populations.

Because parish types differ widely from culture to culture, and even within relatively small areas, it is impossible to provide detailed suggestions which are applicable to all parishes in the future. On the basis of the findings of community and parish studies, however, certain broad observations may be attempted which have general validity.

1. *Adaptability* is an increasingly essential prerequisite of the parish apostolates in modern times. The parish clergy, parochial institutions and services, must be flexible enough to meet sometimes rapidly changing social and cultural conditions. Traditional parish organizations, church services and apostolic techniques must be periodically reviewed and revised to meet the needs of an everchanging parish community. For just as the Church itself, in the words of Pope Pius XII " . . . is a living organism and therefore . . . grows and develops and conforms herself to the requirements and circumstances of various times . . ." [1] so too the parish, which itself is a living cell in the Mystical Body, must maintain itself prepared to adjust its whole apostolate to changing situations.

Adaptability as used here means something more than a mere mechanical compromise with new forces, such as a population invasion or a cultural transformation. It means adoption as well of all that is good in the traditions and values of the prevailing culture. It also means that the parish must accommodate itself in all but essentials to the environment in which it exists to the extent that this accommodation will ultimately further the final objective of every parish, i.e., the salvation of souls within its boundaries. An inflexible identification, by both priests and people, with specific racial or ethnic interpretations of Catholicism, whether it be Irish, French, Polish or other, tends to produce a sterile parish apostolate on our own continent and in mission territories as well. "The Catholic Church" wrote Pius XII, "is not identified with any one culture;

. . . she is ready to enter into relations with all cultures. She recognizes and leaves to subsist whatever in those cultures is not opposed to nature." [2] This ideal of cultural accommodation can only be effectively realized on the parish level. The Holy See has taken the lead on the importance of accommodation and in no area more emphatically than in the development of a native clergy.[3] The work of stimulating and facilitating vocations to the priesthood and religious life is, in the last analysis, a parochial responsibility.

2. *The development or renewal of a parish spirit* is a second essential prerequisite of parishes of all types in modern times. By this is meant an appreciation by clergy and laity for the parish as a community. All too often parishes are looked upon as nothing more than service centers for meeting the religious needs of parishioners and collecting the necessary revenues for the maintenance of the parish plant. For most parishioners it connotes the church, the rectory, the hall, the school, the convent and nothing more. Yet this extremely prevalent interpretation of the nature of a parish is far too restricted. Each parish must be considered a living cell in Christ's Mystical Body. From this it follows that each parish has its own individuality, its principle of spiritual vitality, and its own unity in the spiritual order. That this is a sound interpretation of the parish is abundantly clear from the words of Pope John XXIII in which he quotes directly from a statement of his saintly predecessor, Pope Pius XII:

> The parish is the living cell of a body, that is, the Mystical Body of Christ: it is a living being with a life and breath of its own, with a natural development of its

own and even problems and needs and special sorrows of its own.[4]

This concept of the parish as a spiritual community, as a living organic unity, emphasizes the interrelatedness of all segments of the parish, and the interdependence of all, laity as well as priests and religious, for the achievement of the parish's spiritual goals. The sanctification of the individual parishioner is thus not only the business of the pastor and his assistants, but it is the business of every member of the parish. This point of view, which was apparently well understood by early Christians, has been so diluted by the prevailing spirit of individualism that it is almost incomprehensible to the average Catholic today.[5]

Yet, a revival of this sense of grave responsibility of all parishioners for well-being is particularly necessary in an age, such as ours, characterized especially in urbanized areas by high population mobility, weakened primary group bonds, normlessness, and lack of neighborliness. It is true that the breakdown of natural community clusters, typified by ethnic groupings in national parishes, for example, creates serious obstacles to the development of a true community spirit in the modern parish. Yet it is our contention that this challenge can be and must be met successfully in the interest of a more effective parish apostolate and to provide a solid base for the restoration of sound community values throughout society. It is a theological truism that in human affairs the supernatural is built upon the natural; what is advocated here is that the foundation of a supernatural bond linking parishioners in a special way one to another needs to be reinforced in the natural order by a better understanding of and appreciation for the parish as a sacro-social community. In order to achieve this ideal most completely it certainly will be necessary to emphasize small parishes, rather than the huge parishes now so common. Frequent face to face interactions of parishioners with one another and with parish priests can best be facilitated in parishes that are severely restricted in area and in number of parishioners.

3. Parishes in the future must play *a more active role in the social apostolate* of the Church than they have in the past. Most parishes today function commendably in the all-important practice of charity and almsgiving, and perhaps it is regrettable in some respects that many parish functions in this area have been absorbed by the more efficient centralized Catholic Charities agencies. Yet this *ad hoc* type of parish charitable activity is not enough. Since a parish is the Church in miniature, the local realization of the universal Church, its responsibility in the social apostolate is as broad as that of the Church. The parish is the logical center for the dissemination of the Church's social teaching, as it is the normal channel for the Church's teaching in other areas of faith and morals. Furthermore, the local parish is the logical center for the initiation of social reforms based on the social teachings of the Church. If the magnificent social principles and directives taught by all the great modern pontiffs from Leo XIII through St. Pius X, Benedict XV, Pius XI and XII, and John XXIII, have failed to produce a Christian social revolution, this failure can be traced in large measure to the local parish. For these principles must not only be taught (which they have not been), but they must be interpreted and applied with a view to local social, eco-

nomic and political conditions, and they must be implemented through social action programs designed to meet the needs of the local community.

One of the great tragedies of modern times is the capitulation of so many Christian countries to Communism. This is tragic not only because of the dechristianization and degradation of whole societies, but because these peoples could have been saved for Christ and the Church if the papal social teaching had been propounded and implemented as fearlessly, say, as the Church's teaching on birth control and divorce. The parish today, as never before, is primarily responsible for what some German Catholics of the last century referred to as the "social deaconry" of the Church.[6] The parish is by ecclesiastical prescription the Church's official representative in the world's marketplace. It is only through the persistent and cooperative efforts of parishes that the papal ideal of Christian social reconstruction can be achieved. And, obviously, since the parish clergy are primarily responsible for the dissemination of Catholic doctrine, their training should include a thorough preparation in the social teachings of the Church.

Pope John XXIII strongly urged formation of clergy and laity in the Church's social teachings in his memorable *Mater et Magistra.*

> . . . We must reaffirm most strongly that this Catholic social doctrine is an integral part of the Christian conception of life.
>
> It is therefore Our urgent desire that this doctrine be studied more and more. First of all it should be taught as part of the daily curriculum in Catholic schools of every kind, particularly seminaries, although We are not unaware that in some of these latter institutions this has

been done for a long time now and in an outstanding way. We would also like to see it added to the religious instruction programs of parishes and of associations of the lay apostolate. It must be spread by every means at our disposal: daily newspapers, periodicals, popular and scientific publications, radio and television.

Our beloved sons, the laity can do much to help this diffusion of Catholic social doctrine by studying it themselves and putting it into practice, and by zealously striving to make others understand it.[7]

4. A final recommendation for the parish in the new age, and in many ways the most important recommendation of all, is that there must be a *much greater utilization of lay men and women* in all possible phases of the parish apostolate. The failure of the average parish to exploit to the limit its lay members for the parish apostolate is indeed deplorable. The need is present in every parish, the potential is there, interest and willingness to participate can readily be stimulated in large numbers: what is basically lacking is confidence on the part of priests in the ability of the laity to do the job.

The late Pope Pius XII spoke of the cooperation of the laity as an "indispensable necessity" for the mission of the Church in modern times.[8] Besides, it is apparent from the same Pontiff's 1954 address to the pastors and Lenten preachers of Rome, that one of the primary duties of parish priests is to single out and train lay collaborators in the parish, and to use them in every possible phase of the parish apostolate.[9] It is clearly the mind of the Holy See that the laity, with proper training of course, can and should be used for all apostolic works except those the priest alone can perform because of his priesthood.

The successful utilization of the laity in the parish demands that they be given more freedom and autonomy in their apostolic efforts than is often accorded them. Pope Pius XII clearly recognized the importance of this point in an allocution on the lay apostolate which he delivered in 1951. Speaking of the lay apostle as an "instrument" in the hands of the hierarchy, the Pontiff said that he understood the comparison in this way:

> . . . that the ecclesiastical superiors use him in the manner which the Creator and Lord uses rational creatures as instruments, as second causes. . . . Let them use those instruments, then, with a consciousness of their grave responsibility; let them encourage them, suggesting enterprises to them and welcoming with good will the enterprises which they [lay apostles] suggest, approving them in broadmindedness according to their opportuneness. In decisive battles, it is often at the front that the most useful initiatives arise.[10]

The spirit of many a zealous parishioner has been broken simply because he was not permitted to exercise his own initiative on any important point.

There is yet another facet of the question of lay participation which must be faced realistically. The laity are no longer content to be passive listeners, being called upon to be active only in contributing to the support of the parish and in the performance of certain service tasks. They want to be active participants in the liturgy, for example. Their knowledge and skills are in demand in every phase of community life, but not in the parish. This is the age of the common man, except in the parish apostolate. The Catholic community has an enormous investment in Catholic education, yet there is extreme reluctance to utilize the products of this educational system in the primary mission of the Church—the care of souls. The layman cannot replace the priest in his priestly function, but neither should the priest usurp the rightful prerogative of the laity to share actively in the apostolate of the parish. The success of parishes in this new age depends directly upon an increased and a more intelligent use of the laity in the spiritual mission of the parish.

Inevitably the question arises: What more can the laity do in the parish than they are now doing? This suggests a second question by way of reply: What proportion of the daily life of the average parish priest is devoted to activities and services which he alone can perform because he is a priest? Thirty-five to forty per cent would be a generous estimate on any long term basis. Lay men and women could be trained to replace him in perhaps sixty per cent of his current apostolic efforts, leaving him free to devote one-hundred per cent of his work day schedule to strictly priestly activities. Not only could they lighten his burden immeasurably in the demanding details of business administration for the parish, but they could also, with proper preparation of course, shoulder responsibility for many parish services generally regarded as being priestly activities exclusively.

Convert instructions and all types of counseling services, including marriage counseling, are cases in point. The laity have already demonstrated their ability to function successfully in both areas. Lay organizations such as the Legion of Mary have been overwhelmingly successful in many parishes in shepherding back to the fold countless lost and straying sheep. This approach could be expanded and intensified in the average parish with highly rewarding results. Adult education classes, youth programs, inquiry services of all kinds, parish census work, the manning of parish centers on a twenty-four hour basis, are some of the activities in which the laity have been highly successful on the parish level.

A maximum involvement of lay persons of all ages in the essential mission of the parish is an indispensable key to parish vitality. Lay participation at all possible levels must of necessity promote the sanctification not only of the active apostles but of all, non-Catholics as well as Catholics, who reside within the parish boundaries, while developing a real awareness of the parish as a living community with common goals and shared responsibilities.

The recommendations proposed here for the parish in the new age—greater adaptability and flexibility, the restoration of the parish as a true community, reactivation of the social deaconry role on the parish level, increased utilization of the laity in the parish apostolate—may seem to be radical proposals. Yet, it is the writer's considered judgment that radical changes in the traditional approach to the parish apostolate are clearly indicated if the parish, and the Church, are to meet the challenge of the new age.

NOTES

[1] *Mediator Dei, AAS,* XXXIX (1947), 544.
[2] *Vous avez voulu, AAS* (1955), 681.
[3] See, for example, Pius XII's *Evangelii praecones, AAS,* XLIII (1951), 508.

[4] *L'incontro convoi*, in *Osservatore Romano*, August 17-18, 1962.

[5] For a more complete discussion of this see Thomas J. Harte, "Sociology of the Parish," *Conference Bulletin of the Archdiocese of New York*, XXXV (1958), 16-32, esp. 18-19.

[6] Edgar Alexander, "Church and Society in Germany," *Church and Society*, ed. Joseph N. Moody (New York: Arts, Inc., 1953), pp. 422 ff.

[7] *AAS*, LIII (1961), 453-454.

[8] *De quelle consolation*, *AAS*, XLIII (1951), 784-792.

[9] *Ci sarebbe*, *AAS*, XXXVI (1954), 102.

[10] *AAS*, XLIII (1951).

The Redemption and Morality in the Catholic Family

▶▶

HENRY V. SATTLER, C.SS.R., Ph.D.

Marriage in God

To understand marriage as it ought to be, we cannot be content with the descriptions of the sociologist, the anthropologist, the physician, the historian, or the novelist. Though all these specialists have something to say about marriage and family life which commands our careful attention and study; though the researcher can deepen our knowledge and understanding of the inexhaustible reality which is Marriage and Family Life, we must go to the Author of nature who invented the difference between the sexes and who joined the first couple in marriage in order to understand what marriage is about. In language easily understandable to the primitive chosen people, the very first pages of the Old Testament explain what it is to "marry in God."

In the words of Sacred Scripture, God created each of the wonders in the universe by a simple act of His will, "Let there be Light and light was made." But when it came time to create man, God is pictured as pausing to take counsel within Himself, "Let us make mankind in our image and likeness" (Gn 1,26). "Then the Lord God formed man out of the dust of the ground and breathed into his nostrils the breath of life, and man became a living being." (Gn 2,7)

In all of God's natural creation, God recognized His creation as "good." However, after He had made Adam, the first man, there was no reference to the goodness of His creation. In human terms something was missing. God is pictured as retiring again into Himself to take counsel and consider what next he ought to do, "Then the Lord God said, 'It is not good that man is alone; I will make him a helper like himself.' " (Gn 2,18). So God cast Adam into a deep sleep and formed a woman from his rib, whom he brought to Adam to introduce as his wife. When the first man saw this helpmate, he broke into what is the first poem listed in the pages of Sacred Scripture, "She now is bone of my bone and flesh of my flesh; she shall be called woman for from man she has been taken." (Gn 2,23).

To the young couple, God gave His blessing, or wish for happiness: "Be fruitful and multiply; fill the earth and subdue it." (Gn 1,28).

From this simple little description we can understand the nature of marriage and God. Marriage involves the love of a man and a maid; their determination to be of help to each other; their right to sexual union, and the fruitfulness that flows from it; their duty to change the earth so that it will properly support their family.

By examining the nature of love, the nature of the sexes and the necessity of care for immature children,

human beings can discover all the rules which are necessary in order to insure an effective and happy marriage. If
a union seems to fail, it is not marriage which has failed,
but the two people involved in it. The couple cannot play
God and make up their own rules as they go along. Marriage belongs to God who invented it. It must be played
according to His rules. If a husband and wife decide to
invent their own ground rules, which are in contradiction
to the laws of God for marriage, they should discover
another meaning, another name for their union. It simply
is not marriage, because marriage belongs to God.

This applies not only to the negative laws which pro-
hibit adultery, divorce, contraception, abortion and infanti-
cide, but also to the positive laws, which direct the
thoughtful couple in work together as one principle of
procreation and education. However great may be the
differences with which various cultures work out in detail
the roles of husband and wife, father and mother, the
fundamental functions of provider and director for the
head of the family and of nurse and matrix in the formation of children for the mother, must be followed. The
mutual love and devotion, the division of labor within
and without the home, the different impacts in educative
function must be rediscovered and reapplied in each age
of mankind.

Except in pagan eras, ancient or modern, all cultures
have considered matrimony a state of perfection and a
vocation to serve God through mutual service of each
other and of the children. Marriage is essentially a dedica-
tion to God in the service of new life. This service of new
life is rooted not only in the begetting of children, but

in educating them to new strength, new knowledge, new moral virtues until they reach maturity.

Though marriage has belonged to God from the dawn of creation, human weakness, after the fall of our first parents, has frequently altered, desecrated and all but destroyed the pattern that God had intended. Jesus Christ became Incarnate, not only to restore all things to their rightful order, but also to raise them to a higher level. He came not only to make human beings truly human, but also to make them somewhat divine. Electricity lets the nature of glass and tungsten remain intact, but it transforms them and produces light, which they cannot naturally produce. Similarly, the grace of Christ not only restores full integrity to human nature, but also transforms it in such a way that human beings can produce acts which are truly divine.

The grace of Christ has transformed matrimony in a similar fashion. By the sacrament of matrimony, not only are husband and wife helped to make a more perfect natural marriage, but their marriage is made a divine love affair, without leaving behind any of the natural romance, affection, sexual passion, and deep devotion which belong in marriage. By the sacrament of matrimony Christ transforms all this natural joy of unity into a re-living of the identical love Christ gives His Church and the Church returns to Him.

St. Paul says:

> Let wives be subject to their husbands as to the Lord, because a husband is head of the wife, just as Christ is head of the Church, being Himself Savior of the body. But just

as the Church is subject to Christ, so also let wives be to their husbands in all things.

Husbands, love your wives, just as Christ also loved the Church, and delivered Himself up for her, that He might sanctify her, cleansing her in the bath of water by means of the word; in order that He might present to Himself the Church in all her glory, not having spot or wrinkle or any such thing, but she might be holy and without blemish. Even thus ought husbands also to love their wives as their own bodies. He who loves his own wife, loves himself. For no one ever hated his own flesh; on the contrary he nourishes and cherishes it, as Christ also does the Church (because we are members of His body, made from His flesh and His bones). (Eph 5,21–30).

Here St. Paul is not so much concerned with the subjection of wives to their husbands, the love and devotion that husbands owe their wives, nor even the norm of their mutual devotion, which is the mutual devotion of Christ and His Church. St. Paul is describing here the deep mystery of marriage between two baptized persons, which is an actual living in miniature of the Mystical Body of Christ. In this concept of Christian matrimony the husband takes the place of Christ, and the wife takes the place of the Church. Indeed, they become for each other— Christ loved, and Christ being loved. In this Christian reality, there is no conflict between human love and the love of God. In loving each other in Christian fashion, the spouses love Christ.

The sacramental grace of matrimony divinizes the human unity of natural wedlock. However, it also does more than this. Besides transforming natural marriage it gives special divine helps to make it effective. Christian spouses have the *right* to all the actual graces which will enlighten their minds and move their wills to accomplish the supernatural works of marriage. Further, they have the right to remedial graces which will help them to overcome the cussedness of human nature (which exists because of original sin) and even their weaknesses which flow from past faults and infidelities. As Pope Pius XI says so beautifully:

> . . . Hence this sacrament not only increases sanctifying grace, the permanent principle of supernatural life . . .; but it adds particular gifts, dispositions, seeds of grace, by elevating and perfecting the natural powers in such a way that the parties are assisted, not only in understanding, but in knowing intimately, in adhering to firmly, in willing effectively and successfully putting into practice those things which pertain to the marriage state, its aims and duties. It gives them, in fine, a right to the actual assistance of grace whensoever they need it for fulfilling the duties of their state.

However sublime the concept of Christian marriage in Christ, we must understand that as married people, they have it only *in seed*. God did not want to make us divine from the outside; through His own handiwork He wanted this supernatural living in some way to be the work of our own hands. The seed of divine life, which is grace, and the seed of the Christian concept of matrimony, we must plant and cultivate, weed and prune "in fear and trembling," lest through our own fault we prevent the harvest. Though it is "God who gives the growth," it is for us to "plant" and "water" (1 Cor 3,6), by frequent reception of the sacraments, by constant and daily prayer, especially together within the family, by acts of contrition for daily faults, by daily deep meditative thought on the sublime nature of Christian matrimony. Every married couple must learn to stir up the grace of God which is in them.

The Family in God

All love is creative. When an artist falls in love with the beauty of a sunset, he cannot rest until he has attempted to capture that beauty on canvas. He may destroy effort after effort as being unworthy of his love. He may produce painting after painting, and still feel disappointed that the beauty he conceived has not yet "come to life."

Human love has the same vocation to creativity. First, it creates the real bond of married union. Secondly, in a sometimes spectacular fashion, human love develops an immature boy and girl to rugged responsible virility and warm responsive femininity, maturing in maternity. Thirdly, the rapture of human love wishes to be reflected in children, where parents can see, in the features and physique of their children various reflections of their human love. The natural love of human marriage demands (unless some accident ensue) a family.

The love, the marriage of Christ and His Church, is supernaturally creative. Through His Church, Christ is extended throughout the world in space and time. His Spouse, the Mystical Body, sends His blood pulsing through the world, to every country. Through baptism, she raises up new reflections of His love in every race and color of the universe.

If the union of baptized husband and wife is a miniature Mystical Body; if it is a re-living of Christ's union with His Church within the walls of tiny Christian homes; then it, too, must be supernaturally creative. Christian marriage creates not only a bond of two human wills, but a bond so real and strong that a consummated marriage between baptized persons can never be broken on earth. How could it be broken, since it is the re-living of the same bond which Christ has with His Church, which can never be dissolved? Christian marriage creates spouses, not only mature with the maturity of the natural virtues, but with the deep rich maturity of the supernatural virtues of divine faith, hope and charity; and all the natural virtues transformed by the gifts of the Holy Spirit. Finally, Christian marriage does not merely extend the human race in space and time, it physically extends the Body of Christ through the ages. As the Catholic couple present their newborn infants at the baptismal font—the womb of the Church—they extend the physical Body of Christ through the ages and provide lovers of God, who can love Him with His own kind of love. St. Francis de Sales says that "the purpose of parenthood is to fill the earth with adorers of God and to people heaven with saints."

The historical Christ came to earth at a specific point in historical time, yet He came not merely to redeem the chosen people, or to teach a few chosen souls. He came to contact and redeem every human being upon the earth. Long since, His historical Body has died upon the Cross and gone to heaven, but His Mystical Body remains. If His voice is to be heard in the twentieth century; if His hands are to administer lovingly to the poor, sick and downtrodden of today; if His principles are to transform the world in which we live; He can do this only through the members of His Mystical Body. Though the extension of His Body is the work of all His members, of special pre-eminence is the work of Christian parents, who through the stumbling footsteps, babbling voices and clumsy fingers of their immature children are to provide the voice, the hands, the feet, the mind, the love of Christ to the twentieth century. This is family life in Christ.

Because Christ the Head holds such an eminent position, one must not think that He does not require the help of the Body. What Paul said to the human organism is to be applied likewise to the Mystical Body: "The head cannot say to the feet: I have no need of you." It is manifestly clear that the faithful need the help of the Divine Redeemer, for He has said: "Without Me you can do nothing," and according to the teaching of the Apostle every advance of this Mystical Body toward its perfection derives from Christ the Head. Yet, this, also, must be held, marvelous though it may seem: *Christ has need of His members*. First, because the person of Jesus Christ is represented by the Supreme Pontiff, who in turn must call on others to share much of his solicitude lest he be overwhelmed by the burden of his pastoral office, and must be helped daily by the prayers of the Church. Moreover as our Savior does not rule the Church directly in a visible manner, *He wills to be helped by the members of His Body in carrying out the work of redemption*. This is not because He is indigent and weak, but rather because He has so willed it for the greater glory of His spotless Spouse. Dying on the Cross He left to His Church the immense treasury of the redemption, towards which she contributed nothing. But when those graces come to be distributed, not only does He share this work of sanctification with His Church, but He wills that in some way it be due to her action. This is a deep mystery, and an inexhaustible subject of meditation, that the salvation of many depends on the prayers and voluntary penances which the members of the Mystical Body of Jesus Christ offer for this intention and on the cooperation of pastors of souls and of the faithful, *especially of fathers and mothers of families,* a cooperation which they must offer to our Divine Saviour as though they were His associates. (Pope Pius XII, *Mystici Corporis.* National Catholic Welfare Conference, Washington 5, D.C., para. 44.)

The vocation to Christian parenthood, which is at the heart of Christian family life is a continuing thing. It is not enough to procreate children and so extend the physical Body of Christ. The Latin derivation of the word "parent" means "bring*ing* forth." Pope Pius XI has pointed out that parents are absolutely forbidden to leave undone what they have begun. God does not wish to fill the earth with infants, but with adult men and women. He compliments parents by giving them the development of the children from the moment of conception to the moment when they will completely leave their parents to take up their vocational duties within the Mystical Body of Christ. One might almost say that parenthood involves a period of gestation, not merely of nine months, but of twenty-one years and nine months!

Family life revolves about the instruction and education of children. Most parents accept the responsibility of clothing, feeding and protecting the bodies of their children. But most of them feel that once they have sent them off to school, their function as parents has been pretty well accomplished. No, though our children are physically healthier than ever before in the history of the world, the increase of neurosis and mental illness, the avid pursuit of false philosophy, their inability to enter into social cooperation with their neighbors and their too frequent emptiness of religious experience point out that much more is involved in parenthood.

Family life must teach children how to emote strongly and yet to control and direct the turbulent and undisciplined emotions and passions of youth. Parents must constantly encourage their growing families to pursue the difficult will-of-the-wisp, which is truth. The habitual choice of worthwhile goals to pursue, which is virtue, must be inculcated by word, example, encouragement, reward and punishment. The family must also provide the social experiences of living in which children learn how to share, compete, follow and lead, win and lose. Socially too, they must learn the preeminence of their individual worth and yet the necessity of submerging that value in the cooperation with others.

Christian family life must also teach the child that all these natural values of body, emotion, mind, heart, and social existence must be bound up, dedicated to and transformed by a religious experience. From their earliest days they must learn to say to God the Father: "Thy will be done on earth as it is in heaven." With the Son, they should participate in the sacrifice of the Mass, and suffuse themselves in His grace by the reception of the sacraments. Each year they should relive His life by active participation of the liturgical year.

St. John Chrysostom summarizes this function of family life when he says:

> The art of forming character in the child is far more excellent than the art of the painter or the sculptor. For, whereas they work in paint and marble, he who has

charge of the young works with living flesh and blood.
Their masterpieces consist of canvasses and stone; his
products are living, breathing human beings. It ought to
be an inspiring thought to any Christian parent to realize
that, by wise, consistent discipline, he is able to mold the
souls beautiful in sanctifying grace, masterpieces far above
the most extravagant dreams of any artist.

In all this, father and mother are not merely democratic
members on an equal footing with their children in the
family. Though Christ, His Church, and all Christians are
inextricably woven into the organism of the Mystical
Body, it is Christ who bears full authority, it is the Church
which carries out His commands, and in turn directs the
growth of her children. So also within the Christian
family parents have the very authority of Christ. They
have the duty and, therefore, the right to teach, command
and sanctify each other and their children. Husband and
wife start their mutual sanctification by conferring upon
each other the sacrament of matrimony. They continue this
mutual sanctification and the sanctification of their children by prayer and sacrifice, by mutual encouragement to
participate in the Mass and sacraments, by bringing their
children to the baptismal font, by helping those children
to grow in grace through the sacraments and prayer, by
lovingly correcting each other and their children.

Parents command each other and their children with the
authority of Christ. They can apply to themselves the
words Christ spoke to His Apostles: "He who hears you
hears Me" (Matt 10,40).

The teaching of the truths which God has revealed,
though it can be accomplished in more formal fashion by

priests and religious in Catholic schools, is most effectively taught within the family by authority of parents who *witness* the truth of which they are convinced. St. Paul says: "Faith comes by hearing" (Rom 10,17).

The words of Pope Pius XII prevent us from thinking that these ideas are merely fancy metaphors:

> Through matrimony, in which the contracting parties are ministers of grace to one another, provision is made for the external and duly regulated increase of Christian society, and what is of greater importance, for the correct religious instruction of children, without which the Mystical Body would be in grave danger.

It is not enough to become aware of your family life in Christ. Divine grace does not substitute for the work of our own hands and minds. Therefore, if all we have said above is true, Christian parents, once imbued with a deep sense of their vocation to family life, must first stir up within themselves all the graces of their state. Secondly, they must learn all they possibly can from the sciences about child growth and development. Adult education, study clubs, home and school associations, parent-teacher organizations, are springing up on all sides. Catholics should be in the forefront in their eagerness to deepen their understanding of their function within the family.

Nevertheless the complexity of such knowledge too frequently confuses parents and destroys the very confidence it is meant to supply. Only if the Christian parents are aware that they have available to them the actual graces which will help them to choose wisely from the mass of information in modern natural sciences; only if they are aware that "unless God build the house, they labor in vain, who labor to build it," will they achieve the fullness of family life in God.

The Family at Church

The word "church" is used in many ways. Too frequently Catholics use it to indicate only the church building—the building which houses the faithful when they worship. In this sense the family does have a place at church. In more and more places the family is attending the holy sacrifice of the Mass within the church building *as a family*. In some places this has come about simply because the modern family is "on wheels," and can arrive at the church building only as a unit. But, it has become more and more common that families attend Mass as a unit even when the various members could come at different times. This flows from the greater conviction that the family itself is a Mystical Body which takes its place within the parish family, not through individual attendance, but through its group attendance.

Because of growing awareness of the Mass as a family sacrifice and as a family sacrificial feast, it is becoming customary for the father to lead a discussion on Saturday evening in preparation for Sunday Mass. Since the liturgical year is a yearly re-living of the whole mystery of the Incarnation, many families are living the liturgical year with an increased intensity of their faith. Not only are they aware of the liturgical cycle, but they are introducing home customs built upon their awareness of liturgical life. The Advent Wreath, the Twelve Days of Christmas,

Candlemas, Ash Wednesday and Lenten practices, the Paschal Lamb and many other practices are being embraced with enthusiasm by many families. Many ancient customs are being brought down from the shelves of history, dusted off, modernized and made the *new* customs of the liturgical revival within the family.

As a result of this growing awareness of the place which the family should occupy within the Church, new organizations are springing up, built not upon individual memberships of men, women or youth; not upon the vocational, social or recreational interests of the members, but upon a family awareness. Just as the individual cells in the human body work together for a certain kind of function within an organ; just as these various functions are unified within an organ; just as all the organs work together for the good of the whole—so individuals are beginning to find their natural place within the organism of the family and families are beginning to find their natural place within organizations which recognize the family as the basic unit not only of the civil society, but also of the mystical society which is the Mystical Body of Christ.

However right and proper these new developments must seem to those of us who are aware of family needs today, they are merely external indications of a deeper awareness of the family's place at the church in another sense. In this sense "Church" means "the household of the faith." It refers to all those who are joined by baptism and faith to Christ within His Mystical Body. In this meaning "Church" does not mean a building or a highly centralized organization, it means an organism. *Within this organism* the family has a far more important place than it has within the church as a building. Indeed its place within the church building is merely symbolic of the deeper meaningfulness.

In the human body it is not so much the mouth that eats, nor the stomach that assimiliates, it is an entire functioning person. In the same way the assimilation of all mankind into ultimate unity with Christ within His Body, is the function of the entire physical Body and not merely the special duty of bishops and priests. Christ gave to His entire infant Church the commission "Go, therefore, and make disciples of all nations, baptizing them in the name of the Father, and of the Son, and of the Holy Spirit, teaching them to observe all that I have commanded you" (Matt 28,30). The Apostles and their successors, the bishops, are primarily responsible for this commission, but all Christians are members of Christ's Body and Christ speaks to them also in giving this command. Every individual within the Church is touched by this commission, but the family is especially involved in the apostolate of the Church to the whole world.

In the broad sense the apostolate of the family can be comprised in the apostolates of prayer, of suffering, and of good example. Within the apostolate of prayer, as you adore, praise, thank, propitiate and petition God, you are opening the floodgates of divine grace to the whole world. It is only necessary then to extend your personal prayer to include not only your own needs and the needs of your family but also the needs of friends, community, nation, enemies and the world. Pope Pius XII points out how this can be within the family, when he says:

> But the apostolic spirit takes root in the heart of the child, not only at school, but long before school age and

is engendered by the care of the mother herself. The child will learn how to pray at Mass and offer the Sacrifice with an intention which embraces the whole world and, above all, the important interests of the Church. Examining his conscience concerning his duties toward his neighbor, he will not only ask himself, "Have I done harm to my neighbor," but will also ask, "Have I shown him the way which leads to God, to Christ, to the Church, and to salvation?"

At first sight it would seem that we cannot add to the sufferings of Christ in saving the world. However, Christ has ordained that though His Merits are waiting for our use, He will not release them into the world until we join His Body in suffering. St. Paul remarks, "I rejoice now in the suffering I bear for your sake; and what is lacking of the sufferings of Christ, I fill up in my flesh for His Body, which is the Church" (Col 1,24). It is hard to suffer alone, it is difficult to join one's personal suffering to those of Christ unless there is a community which helps one to do so. If we would like all our children to continue Christ's Crucifixion through sniffles, chicken pox, chores, studies and obedience; if we could harness to the Cross our own aches and pains, as we grow older; if we could persuade the aged to add their arthritic pangs and their boredom to the sufferings of the Cross, we would soon convert the world.

Our Protestant friends urge their members to *witness* to the love of Christ, while too often we depend upon preaching to win converts. Far more convincing is Catholic family life lived so that all can see. St. Paul says, "Faith comes by hearing" (Rom 10,17). He means to say that conversions from unbelief to belief, from bad life to good life come chiefly from observing the conviction with which Catholics witness to the truths they hold. Families cannot "hide their light under the measure," they must put it "upon the lamp stand, so as to give light to all in the house" (Matt 5,15). This does not mean that families should become boasting, aggressive, hypocritical or showy, but simply that they live their Christian family life with such joy and enthusiasm that anyone who cares to see will be affected. This is another reason for joining one of the numerous family groups which are springing up. By mutual good example of family members, such groups make an impact on the local parochial community of far greater weight than the sum total of their individual members.

Besides the apostolates of prayer, suffering and example, the most immediate apostolate open to Christian parents is to take the place of Christ within their own homes. In begetting children, they extend the Mystical Body which is the purpose of every apostolate. In teaching their children they perform the function of Christ as King, Teacher and Priest. Happy families make other happy families. Their home provides a school for family living in which children learn by observation and identification the roles of husband and wife, father and mother. They are trained to start other organisms within Christ's Body, as they mature and ready themselves for marriage.

The family also provides priestly and religious vocations in the Western Church. Since celibacy is the rule for clerics, the Church cannot multiply its bishops and priests from among the clergy. It must look to the families. At the present time there is a great shortage of priests, brothers, sisters. Christ has not and cannot desert His Spouse the

Church. He certainly has called enough of her children to "come follow Me." But His call has been silenced because vocations are not being fostered within Christian families. In the home in which a young man or woman learns love of God and man, the meaning of sacrifice and generosity, the development of virtue, discipline of one's own unruly desires, this is what produces and fosters the call of God. Canon Cardijn says:

> The humblest of laboring man should regard his home life as an apostolate out of which Church and nation may draw the priests, missionaries and apostles they need. For the basic ideal of family life is to "multiply the number of the elect" (Canon Cardijn, *The Spirit of the Christian Workers,* Catholic Truth Society, Toronto, p. 13).

I must add a reminder here, that though the vocation of celibacy in clergy or cloister is a special call from God, there is also a true vocation to the single state in the secular world. Many dedicated people are remaining unmarried by choice in order to devote themselves to the service of mankind and of God in special works which may be more or less closed to the strictly religious life. Real awareness and respect for the single state in the world should be included in the educative function of all families, so that all children approach their callings in marriage or in celibacy, the single state, with a real sense of Christian accomplishment.

In a stricter sense, families can partake of a lay apostolate within the Church. It is not fully true that the lay apostolate is necessary today because we have an insufficient number of bishops, priests and nuns. True, an active lay apostolate can do some substitutional work with the paucity of vocations. With proper commission, lay people can teach catechism, practice the corporal and spiritual works of mercy within such organizations as the Legion of Mary and the St. Vincent DePaul Society. They can spread the word of God directly through Catholic newspapers and religious programs on radio and television.

However, the lay apostolate is concerned not only to transform individuals whom they meet and convert them to active Catholicism, but it must also transform the instituitions, customs and practices of the community. Bishops and priests should not enter into party politics, labor disputes, civic administration or the Christian practice of professions such as medicine and law. Yet if Christ is to be heard in legislative halls, He must be heard through the voices of Christian politicians. This is equally true for the professions of medicine and law, for work fields such as carpentry and plumbing, for labor management problems, for school boards and town meetings, for all international diplomacy and organizations. The only way Christ can enter into these public affairs is through an informed lay people who are aware of the fullness of the apostolate to which they are called. Pope Pius XII says:

> The consecration of the world is essentially the work of the laymen themselves, of men who are intimately a part of the economic and social life, who participate in the government and in legislative assemblies. In the same manner, the Catholic cells which must be created among workers in every factory and in all the working environments for bringing back to the Church those who have strayed from Her, can be constituted only by the workers themselves (Discourse of His Holiness Pope Pius XII to the Second World Congress for the Lay Apostolate).

Of particular value within the lay apostolate are those groups which center their organization about the family. The impact of family upon family can be greater than the impact of their heads or hearts (father or mother). In some sense the best teachers of Christian marriage should be Christian families, since they are professionally living in Christian marriage and have their own sacrament. Again, since the family feels the impact of social change upon itself as a unit, and not only upon isolated members, families together can more easily transform their neighborhoods into such community awareness that a Christian family life is not only possible, but even promoted.

The Church in the Family

Father Mersch has entitled his book on the Mystical Body *The Whole Christ*. The whole Christ comprises Christ, the Pope, all the bishops, diocesan and religious clergy, religious orders of brothers and nuns, and lay people gathered (at least in majority) in families. St. Paul points out that in Christ there is no longer male or female, slave or free, but all are Christ's and Christ's are God's. Therefore, there is no distinction in membership though there is difference in function.

Christ and His Church as one unit have always been concerned for the fullness of marriage and family life. During His lifetime Christ restored the unity and indissolubility of marriage by condemning adultery, fornication, polygamy and even lustful thoughts. He concerned Himself for the material well-being of the young couple at the wedding feast in Cana. Though the time is not clear in Scripture, he raised natural marriage to the dignity of a sacrament.

Holy Mother Church has been equally vigilant. The writings of the fathers of the church would fill volumes if we selected only those passages which referred to marriage and family life. The popes, through the centuries, have clarified doctrinal points about marriage. Ecclesiastical law has always regulated the unions of the faithful.

All Christian doctrine unfolds through the centuries as rosebud into rosebloom. In almost every case doctrine has been clarified and developed to meet attacks upon it. The divinity and humanity of Christ were defined on two separate occasions when heretics proposed that Christ was divine, but not human; or again, human but not divine. So it is with the doctrine on matrimony. The Council of Trent defined that matrimony was one of the seven sacraments, when the Reformers denied it. More recently the false notions of free love, easy divorce, the amorality of pre-marital sexual experience, the increase of abortion-murders, etc. have provoked from the teaching-body of the Church many clarifications on the nature of matrimony. It has remained for our day to fully develop a more positive doctrine on Christian matrimony. The encyclicals of Pope Leo XIII and Pius XI are the classic theoretical developments. Pope Pius XII taught the practical function of marriage and family life so voluminously that a whole lifetime would not be enough to learn the full implication of his doctrine.

Following the lead of these recent Pontiffs more books have been written by Catholic authors on marriage and family in the past twenty years than have appeared in an equivalent time in the entire history of the Church. In my own lifetime this can be verified. When I first began work on marriage and the family it was difficult to find twenty good Catholic works in English. Today, the list includes two hundred titles! Yes, the Church will always be concerned for the fundamental organism within the Mystical Body which is the family.

Yet, much remains to be done. Doctrinally there are many areas that need investigation by theologians who must in turn pass on their discoveries to priests, teachers, counselors, and leaders. Though we know that matrimony is a sacrament, we are not certain about the function of sacramental grace in matrimony. In Canon law, our matrimonial courts decide upon validity and nullity of marriage. But further clarifications must be sought from the Holy See, for example on the sacramental marriages of the dubiously baptized and the application of the Pauline Privilege and the Privilege of the Faith.

Moral theologians must explore more deeply the morality of the various conjugal obligations. The immorality of abortion, contraception and divorce is quite clear. But the morality of the mutual obligations to the *debitum*, the extent of a wife's obedience to her husband, the responsible use of the rhythm, the areas of children's dependence upon parents are by no means as detailed as they might be.

For centuries, ascetical theology has been written for the cloistered celibates. The entire virtue system of St. Thomas and the applicability of the gifts of the Holy Ghost must be rethought to show how they may apply to the daily living of family life. The counsels of poverty, chastity and obedience which, we glibly say, must be pursued by all Christians, should be reduced to achievable goals which a harassed mother or father may pursue.

Philosophically, the whole concept of the natural law upon which we build most of our knowledge must be re-thought to meet the needs of modern living. The psychological discoveries on the nature and growth of human love must be integrated into the classic analysis by St. Thomas. The philosophical awareness of masculinity and feminity must keep pace with modern research on sexual differences.

As we become more aware of the social fabric and re-act against individualism, as we meditate on the supernatural community, the Mystical Body of Christ, we must re-discover the family as the basis of society.

The science of sociology is bringing to light many of the needs which the family has in order to remain healthy. Catholic teaching must take into consideration the exigencies of housing, the pressures of "group-think" mentality, the anxieties of family insecurity, the loss of identification with cultural groups due to family mobility, the gradual disappearance of the rural family, the longer years needed to educate children, the costs of maintaining health, the causes of juvenile and adult delinquency, the spiritual, psychological, and physical problems of the aging.

Family law is almost non-existent in the United States. Catholic leaders must begin to take a lead not only in developing more uniform laws regarding marriage, divorce and separation, but also on those legal involvements which affect the stability of marriage, such as property rights, the legal rights of parents and their children, the control of obscenity and sexual perversion.

If one can judge from published utterances by leaders of labor, business, professional and political organizations, it would seem that they treat their members as though they were celibates! If the Church is to be fully operative in the family, it must provide Christian leadership which gives more than lip service to the family as the basic unit of society. There are Christian spokesmen for farmers, manufacturers, labor and other special interest groups. Where are the spokesmen for the family?

It is not enough to encourage the best thought and research from all the disciplines which can help the family. Our practical work and our Catholic institutions must come to the defense of the family which is attacked from all sides.

In our concern for the building and development of a Catholic school system, have we unconsciously persuaded parents to abdicate their responsibility for the Christian education of their children? Have we subtly suggested that a degree in education is the only thing which will fit a person to perform the function of educator for children? Is there some truth in the complaint of many parents that they are treated as intruders when they wish to discuss their children's progress with their teachers?

In our diocesan and parochial organization have we forgotten all about the family? Do the meetings of our men's, women's, youth and professional organizations tend to atomize the family? Though we can preach more easily to children at a children's mass and check Mass attendance of children whose parents are careless, has this selectivity of the child been done to make it easier for us and thereby unconsciously encourage the very lack of responsibility we decry? I do not say that groups of men, women, and children which meet separately from each other are necessarily bad or without impact on the family; I do not say that the modern cult of "togetherness" is altogether good. I do not deny that men and women and children have different interests. I simply say that the question must be asked if the family is to develop into the militant organism it should be. To me it is an anomaly that our diocesan organizations should have well staffed offices on chancery procedures, building programs, health and hospitals, Catholic school systems, Catholic Charities, Confraternity of Christian Doctrine, Propagation of the Faith, etc., while few have truly effective family life programs.

No doubt, all of our work within Catholic parochial and diocesan organizations have beneficial impact upon families, but are we so concerned with *auxiliary services* to the family that we have forgotten the *direct* and *immediate support* of those families? The following objectives are recommended as immediately necessary if we are to prevent further ravages made by seculars in our family life and if we are to build positively good families and through them build up the Mystical Body of Christ:

1. Adequate marriage preparation must be provided for all young people entering marriage, whether individually, or in groups, or by correspondence. Marriage preparation must become universal.

2. Those already married must be helped to achieve and retain a vision of Christian family life which will sustain them throughout the many dark moments of their lives. Though it is important to preach missions which will bring before people their sins against marriage and

family life, it is even more important to provide them with the motivation which will enable them to at least strive to incorporate the values of a fully Christian family life into their own homes. To this end, Cana conferences, family missions, evenings of recollections, family holy hours and family retreats must be made available to the people. Personally, I am convinced that a high percentage of Catholic families are hungry for the fullness of family spirituality. Even the worst of families will respond to the Christian challenges, if only we can reach them and make them listen.

3. Families must gather together in some kind of mutual support, whether their gatherings take the form of Cana clubs, Mr. and Mrs. Clubs, family cooperatives, Cana Sodalities, etc.; families need to meet and encourage each other. They must also continue their education, so that in the complex modern world they can properly form the attitudes they need to face the times in which they live.

4. No matter how hard we strive, we will not be able to reach every Catholic family by the methods so far outlined. We must use our wonderful means of modern communication to reach them. Though massive demonstrations may not seem to accomplish much, they do have their value in bringing Christian family values to the attention of the community at large. Radio, television, newspapers (Catholic and secular), pamphlets, magazines, and books must be utilized to make men and women better husbands and wives, fathers and mothers.

5. In the best of families, family life does not always move smoothly. It becomes more and more apparent that family counseling services are needed in every diocese not only to prevent unnecessary divorces and separations; not only to help the disintegrating family; not so much to provide remedial care, but to provide

preventive family medicine. Many a festering sore of discontent could be cured before it becomes a destructive cancer; many areas of apparent disunity could form the basis for deeper real unity, if only the couple were helped in time.

The above should not be interpreted as pessimistic! Though there remains much to be done, a tremendous amount has already been accomplished. Our good Catholic families of today are better families than they were a generation ago, because they are striving with a full consciousness for real sanctity, without the support of the national customs of their grandparents. They are living a life, not of resignation to, but joyful acceptance of the patterns of Christian living. Here is the challenge which so many families are now taking up. For the first time in the history of the Church they are in the process of building a Christian pattern of family living based solely upon Catholic insight and principles and not merely upon the encrusted and fading cultures of the past. Modern Catholic family life can now be built by an educated Catholic laity upon clear, conscious insightful choices, based upon a deepening Catholic theology of marriage. Many families are making conscious and explicit what has so long remained latent and implicit in the inexhaustible treasures of Catholic doctrine. They are the Giant Mystical Body, stirring, awakening, stretching its limbs. *Soon* they will be strong and healthy. Soon they will begin as lay-people in the vocation of Christian matrimony to draw their neighbors to wonder, to question and to join the growing Body. Soon—perhaps —through them, there will be but one flock and one shepherd.

The Import of Self-Concept and Self-Ideal in the Life of the Gifted Child

▶▶

WILLIAM F. JENKS, C.SS.R., Ph.D.

It might be well to start off with a clear understanding of what we mean by a gifted child. Paul Witty's definition is quite generally accepted today.[1] He includes in it not only those children with high intelligence, but also "those whose performance in any valuable line of human activity is consistently or repeatedly remarkable."

Some authors do not agree with Witty's definition. Professor Leta S. Hollingworth would define the gifted as children who are in the top one per cent of the general population in general intelligence. She defines general intelligence as the "power to achieve literacy and to deal with its abstract knowledge and symbols."[2] The term "academically talented" which is gaining currency in educational circles, is defined by Conant as the top fifteen to twenty per cent of high school students, "the group who should be going to college." [3]

Depending upon your definition of "gifted children" and upon the criteria you use to identify them, impressingly large numbers of school-age children fall within the group of talented youth. Based upon the revised Stanford-Binet scale and assuming a school population of thirty million, the upper one per cent of that population would give us 300,000 gifted children. Setting the lower limit at 130 IQ, four per cent of the school population, or 1,200,000 may be classified as gifted. And if, as in Cleveland, the cutting-off point is set at 125 IQ, then there would be six and one-half per cent or 1,950,000 gifted children in the United States. The National Manpower Council and the National Education Association estimate that 400,000 bright children each year are being denied a chance to develop their potential.[4]

At the University of Chicago an inquiry was made into the different meanings and values attached to the idea of giftedness by the several groups in our society most involved in the adolescent's life—his parents, his teachers and his peers.[5]

Among the conclusions was the fundamental finding that most gifted students, often described as the nation's hope for the future, fall into one of two categories—"those who are highly intelligent but not so highly creative, and those who are highly creative but not so highly intelligent."[6]

Questioning both parents and teachers of various gifted students, the investigators found that:

1. Teachers hold a great preference for the student with high intelligence and less creativity—the one with a high IQ but less imagination.

2. Parents prefer the gifted child who tends toward creativity, but with a bit lower IQ—the one who exhibits more traits of "good moral character and social skill."

The relevant findings may be summarized as follows: (1) Although teachers and parents defined the gifted child in the same terms, teachers appear to *want* gifted children in the classroom; parents appear *not* to want them in the family; (2) The relationship between qualities defining giftedness in children and qualities believed to be essential for success in adult life is *nil* for teachers, somewhat higher but still low for parents; (3) The personal aspirations of children themselves are generally unrelated to their teachers' and parents' definitions of giftedness.

"The Outstanding Traits Test was administered to approximately 450 high school students who were asked to rank the different children 'on the degree to which you would like to be like them.' These rankings of what might be called the *self-ideal* of children were then compared with the rankings already obtained from teachers and parents. The correlations varied for boys and girls, for teachers and for parents, but they were uniformly *low*—no correlation exceeded 0.30, and two were negative. For example, the first three qualities selected by girls as those they would like for themselves were social skill, moral character, and emotional stability. High marks, IQ, and creativity ranked toward the bottom." [7]

It is interesting to note that both teachers and parents held IQ, high marks and creativity as the qualities most characteristic of giftedness. It seems from this study that some talented children do not want to be gifted. They would much rather be successful. With proper guidance, the talented student could be led to perceive giftedness as a road to success and security, and could be helped to free himself from his erroneous concepts of giftedness.

The Idea of Self-Concept and Self-Ideal

The attitude taken by the gifted students in this recent study at the University of Chicago might well explain the lack of the proper self-concept and the lack of the self-ideal which could result in underachievement and lack of motivation on the part of talented students.

In the life of the gifted child there are two factors which play a very important part; namely, the child's *self-concept* and the child's *self-ideal*. A child's self-concept is the picture of himself which he has been constructing from his very early years. Some gifted children unfortunately think of themselves as "only an average boy," or "a boy whom nobody cares much about." [8]

The gifted child should have a *self-ideal*—a special niche in this world which he would like to fill. Bernard Shaw said that his happiness began when he focused his attention on the things he could do and ignored those in which he was likely to fail. [9] When a talented student conforms to average standards, there is a serious loss of human resources, and conforming for the sake of popularity with one's peers results in reduction to mediocrity. If others recognize and accept the gifted child's true abilities, this helps the child to accept himself and his strengths and limitations.

Self-Concept

Ruth Strang emphasizes the importance of the self-concept when she writes that the development of a child is influenced by the manner in which he perceives himself, and that education has the responsibility of aiding the child to develop a clearer idea of his most acceptable self and to guide him in the development of that acceptable self. She claims that parents and teachers influence the child's concept of himself. The child tends to live up to the labels which he receives from others: lazy, dull, mean, helpful, bright or good.[10]

Carl Rogers claims that most of the ways of behaving which are adopted by the organism are those which are consistent with the concept of self.[11] As for example, "the man who has certain values attached to honesty cannot strive for a sense of achievement through means which seem to him dishonest. . . . Of the various ways of satisfying the need for food or for affection, the individual selects only those which are consistent with the concept which he has of himself." [12]

Ruth Strang claims that a child's concept of himself is built on the chemistry of the body and the structure and functions present at birth.[13] The child gradually gains the ability to relate and organize experience, and is influenced by approval and disapproval, praise and blame, acceptance and rejection. According to Sullivan, an individual's personality is built out of the complex of interpersonal relations in which he lives.[14] Through experiences with his mother he develops a concept of himself. Sullivan has described the possible kinds of self-concepts as the *Good-me*, the *Bad-me*, and the *Not-me*. When the self-system is involved, any individual tries to learn quickly in order to keep a feeling of security and to maintain his concept of himself.[15] Mead, Cooley, Angyal, Lecky and others have helped to advance our knowledge of the development and functioning of the self.

During his preschool years the child's concept of himself is largely determined by his interpersonal relations with parents, brothers and sisters, playmates and other persons with whom he comes in contact. These persons either help him to find himself by giving him freedom to be himself and learn what he can do, or they contribute to his "loss of self" by trying to change his ways of behavior and by maintaining a critical attitude, which gives him the impression that he is "bad, worthless and unloved." [16]

A child's learning is influenced by his concept of himself. If he puts no value on himself or thinks of himself as a failure, he meets each learning situation limply; he has no zest for learning. He begins to value himself as teachers call attention to his strong points and he senses that he is liked and respected by persons important in his life. As a rule, a child usually resists learning anything that is not in accord with his concept of himself. As experiences occur in his life, according to Ruth Strang, he tends to perceive and organize them in relation to his self-concept. If the experience is a threat to his self-esteem, he may deny or distort it.[17]

Carl R. Rogers in his book entitled *Client-Centered Therapy* writes about the construct of self in client-centered therapy. "The client felt he was not being his real self, often felt he did not know what his real self was, and felt satisfaction when he had become more truly himself." [18] Rogers suggests a definition of self-concept based on clinical experience and research evidence that reads like this: "The self-concept or self-structure may be thought of as an organized configuration of perceptions of the self which are admissible to awareness. . . . It is composed of such elements as the perceptions of one's characteristics and abilities; the precepts and concepts of the self in relation to others and to the environment; the value qualities which are perceived as associated with experiences and objects; and goals and ideals which are perceived as having positive or negative valence." [19]

Influence of School and Parents on Talented Youth

Behavior problems among gifted children are of interest to us, and the home and the school are considered the primary causes of maladjustment. The general impression has been that gifted children are unpopular. Barbe found that in heterogeneous classes of children in grades four to seven, bright children were chosen by the average child in the class far more frequently than were the slow learners.[20]

In a school situation where their talents are not challenged, gifted children are frustrated and not only do poor work in their subjects, but cause disturbances by talking back to their teachers and acting smart. Gifted preadolescent children should have a moderate measure of individual freedom to suggest special projects and to set goals for themselves.

Some parents exert pressure on their talented child and force him to perform up to certain standards, or to exhibit social or emotional maturity that he has not yet reached. They may regard him as a prodigy and display him as such.

The school should help the parents to accept both aspects of their child; namely, that he is a child and that he is gifted. Parents should be made to understand that motivation and encouragement are not synonymous with pressure.

Parents should assist their talented children in focusing on their self-ideal, and help them to work within their limitations up to their potential.

Self-Ideal

Dom Thomas Verner Moore states that whatever convinces one of his excellence and importance ". . . awakens a satisfaction which once experienced is ever afterwards craved and so constitutes a powerful driving force of human nature." [21] Anything that enhances the self-ideal may lead to feelings of self-confidence, whereas anything that leads in the opposite direction, or threatens to do so, may cause depression, gloom, "feelings of inferiority," discouragement or fear.

Dom Moore claims that the *self-ideal* is one's own private, personal opinion of one's self, of (a) one's present abilities, and (b) what one hopes to attain. He says that it varies enormously with the intelligence of the individual. It has no existence in the idiot, little or none in the imbecile, but is definitely present in the moron, who often overestimates himself and what he can do.

Moore goes on to say that the factors that determine the self-ideal are: (1) *Accidents of the environment.* A child's idea of himself and his future life is often built upon parental example. The child's teacher and others with whom he comes in contact influence him also. The influence of sermons, lectures and books are of secondary importance to the personal influence of example and verbal appeal. (2) *Hereditary abilities.* Along with the accidents of environment, hereditary abilities are factors in determining not only what we are and what we want to be but also what we think we are. Success pleases and satisfies; failure causes chagrin and discontent. (3) *Organ inferiority.* Alfred Adler developed the idea that the choice of a career depends not upon one's native abilities but upon some hereditary disability. An individual who has an inferior organ realizes more or less painfully his disability. This realization gives rise to a feeling of inferiority which lowers his personal self-esteem. This conflicts with a tendency present in everyone to elevate his own personal self-estimation. The individual then creates for himself an ideal end in which he excels in the very ability in which he is deficient, and his whole life becomes henceforth an attempt to dominate in the very field of his disability. Adler points out historical examples in confirmation of this view: for example, the deafness of Beethoven, the stammering of Demosthenes.[22]

Motivation

"Academic accomplishments of the gifted depend upon complex interrelationships of intelligence, personality, identification with social-class values, peer relationships, parental environment, and school milieu. What are the specific factors of motivation, achievement, and underachievement which determine academic success or failure?" [23]

Wilson discussed motivation and stressed the fact that

the gifted are more strongly motivated than intellectually average children, and related such motivation to the unique qualities of giftedness.[24]

Motivation is the spark plug of learning, according to Strang.[25] A motive is identified by the specific kinds of goals which it involves. The ego-drive—the desire to maintain self-esteem—is a strong motive for learning. The gifted child should be motivated to reach his self-ideal and to use his God-given talents to the best of his ability. This theory of learning has been extensively dealt with by Ernest R. Hilgard.[26] Gowan, in reviewing a number of unpublished studies, discovered that twice as many boys as girls were underachievers and recommended male counselors for the boys. The background of the underachiever showed parental rejection and hostility.[27]

One of the greatest social wastes in our culture today is that presented by the talented child or young person who either cannot or will not work up to his or her ability. Counseling these young people presents a challenging and important problem for teachers and personnel workers. We may define underachievement in general as performance which places the individual 30 percentiles or more below his ability standing in the same group.

Some of the findings of Gowan's study are as follows: [28] The basic causes of the gifted children's behavior and underachievement as diagnosed by the clinic staff were:

1. Disagreement between the parents, and of the parents with their own parents, over methods of rearing the child.

2. Transference of problems of parents to the child.

3. Overanxiety or overprotectiveness on the part of the parents.

4. Fears of parents regarding child's health or safety.

5. Divorces or separations of parents.

6. Parents' failure to prepare child for the birth of a new baby.

Counseling and Guidance

Many of the studies on talented youth deal with psychological and educational factors, but scant attention has been given to counseling procedures. A new study, *Project Talent*, which has tested almost a half million high school students, a five per cent nationally representative sample of the nation's high school youth, should reveal very valuable data, since the directors of the guidance programs and each counselor filled out a questionnaire and made comments on the goals and functions of their guidance program.[29]

In the field of guidance it is very important that the counselor or the teacher knows how the student perceives himself. Frequently the child's self-concept will vary considerably from the facts which are indicated from the test results.[30] Ruth Strang poses some questions for the teacher and the counselor to consider in guiding a gifted child: "What is his self-concept, his idea of himself? Does he think of himself as inferior, worthless, inadequate? Does he feel loved? Does he feel understood? Is he more self-centered than other children of his age usually are? Is he dissatisfied with his appearance, his school ability, his social ability?" [31]

Because of the problems encountered by talented students, some may be in greater need of guidance services than many of their average classmates. An enriched guidance program is greatly needed for our talented youth. If trained counselors cannot be made available, a guidance program can be developed with classroom teachers.

Formerly, many gifted students never knew that they had special endowments simply because educators feared that they might become conceited. This attitude on the part of educators might be responsible for the lack of self-concept and self-ideal by many gifted students. Today there seems to be quite general agreement that talented students should be informed of their abilities. Proper guidance can help them to see that more is expected of them on account of their gifts. Awareness of especially high abilities should be an incentive to the realization of their full potential, and the conviction that with these gifts goes a responsibility both to society and to themselves to develop them fully.

DeHaan and Havighurst feel that one-half of the most able students "do not continue their training to the point where their talent is fully developed." [32] These talented students lack the self-ideal which would lead them to college and university due to lack of motivation. They settle for less than they can aspire to on account of lack of self-ideal. The incentive to pursue his education could be aroused in the student by a competent guidance counselor.

Oftentimes, the community, the home or the school climate of opinion do not always respect special abilities.

The guidance counselor can do much to mold the climate of public opinion and make academic ability respected.

Adequate motivation is probably at the core of much of the problems of providing for talented students. Insufficient motivation, and the lack of self-concept and self-ideal seem to be reasons why so much of our potential resources are not developed to the maximum. The correlation between intellectual ability and achievement could probably be broken down into the four following factors: (1) *Need for achievement.* DeHaan and Havighurst feel that "where it exists, it takes the form of wanting to do one's best at anything or almost anything one tries. It causes a generally high aspiration level." [33] This can be traced to family experience. (2) *Valuing of achievement.* This also can be traced to the high value which mothers and fathers place on achievement. (3) *Intrinsic motivation.* These persons derive great pleasure from their work because they have grown to like it and look for no external reward or approval. (4) *Social motivation.* It is the "social expectation that operates to make a gifted child want to develop his abilities." [34] This is closely related to the climate of opinion which is derived from parents, community, teachers and peers. (5) *The school* with the proper guidance personnel can inspire talented pupils to work towards their potential.

Cutts and Moseley have advanced three generalizations concerning achievement of talented children. First, high achievers are more likely to have made a definite career choice and thus are working toward some goal. In other words, they have a self-ideal. Secondly, they are more likely to be accelerated by a year or two. This has two consequences—they feel they have a reputation to live up to, they meet a more appropriate challenge and thus enhance their self-concept. Thirdly, they are more likely to have somewhat studious parents who set an example of intellectual activity which tends to motivate any talented child.[35]

Conclusion

One of the major problems confronting this nation today is that of manpower shortage, particularly in technical and professional fields. Since all of this potential manpower passes through the nation's schools, educators have the prime responsibility for uncovering talent. In the school year 1956-57 almost 36,000 students in the ninth and tenth years of the senior high schools in New York City had the Iowa Tests of Educational Development administered to them. In one high school approximately 50 per cent of the high ability students in the ninth year (IQ 130 or higher) were not functioning at expected levels of achievement in their school work. The New York City school system and the Columbia School of Engineering devised plans for the "Talent Preservation Project" which investigated these shortages and the manner in which they relate to school underachievement on the part of the gifted.[36]

June of 1959 marked the mid-point of the project. Significant findings disclosed the impact that the investigation made on the schools, the parents, and above all, on the students themselves. Most significant was the awakening of student interest by the mere fact of identification—the recognition of potentiality by another. Many gifted students were unaware of their superior abilities and were not planning further education. Changed attitudes about their education and careers resulted. Their self-concept and their self-ideals were enhanced, and this sparked their motivation.

And so, we must conclude that it is vitally important for talented students to be identified as early as possible, to arrive at their proper self-concept, and be motivated toward their self-ideal according to their potentialities. From the writings of the various authors, it is quite clear that the self-concept of a person is the personality of that person as he perceives it.

Much research is still needed in order to determine whether pupils with high IQ who are high achievers differ significantly in self-concept from pupils with high IQ who are low achievers. A study of the sex of the pupils involved would be very interesting. The influence of the teachers and parents on average IQ pupils who are high achievers, and their self-concept and self-ideal as compared with pupils with high IQ who are high achievers would make a very interesting research study.

NOTES

[1] Paul Witty, "Education Programs for the Gifted," *School and Society,* LXXXVII (April 11, 1959), p. 167.
[2] Leta S. Hollingworth, "How Should Gifted Children Be Educated?," *Baltimore Bulletin of Education,* L (May, 1931), p. 195.
[3] National Education Association, "An Introductory Statement," *The Identification and Education of the Academically Talented Student in the American Secondary School* (Washington, D.C.: The Association, 1958), p. 16.
[4] National Education Association, *Administration: Procedures and*

School Practices for the Academically Talented Students in the Secondary School (Washington, D.C.: The Association, 1960), p. 15.

[5] J. W. Getzels and P. W. Jackson, "The Study of Giftedness: A Multidimensional Approach," *The Gifted Student, Cooperative Research Monograph* (Washington, D.C.: U.S. Government Printing Office, 1960).

[6] *Ibid.*, p. 1.

[7] *Ibid.*, p. 5.

[8] Ruth Strang, *Helping Your Gifted Child* (New York: Dutton & Co., 1960), p. 46.

[9] *Ibid.*, p. 46.

[10] Ruth Strang, *An Introduction to Child Study* (New York: Macmillan Co., 1951).

[11] Carl R. Rogers, *Client-Centered Therapy* (Boston: Houghton Mifflin Co., 1951), p. 507.

[12] *Ibid.*, p. 508.

[13] Strang, *loc. cit.*, p. 458.

[14] Harry Stack Sullivan, *The Interpersonal Theory of Psychiatry* (New York: W. W. Norton & Co., 1953).

[15] *Ibid.*, pp. 161-64.

[16] Strang, *loc. cit.*, p. 198.

[17] Strang, *loc. cit.*, p. 417.

[18] Carl R. Rogers, *Client-Centered Therapy* (Boston: Houghton Mifflin Co., 1951), p. 136.

[19] *Ibid.*, pp. 136-137.

[20] Walter B. Barbe, "Peer Relationships of Children of Different Intelligence Levels," *School and Society*, LXXX (August 21, 1954), pp. 60-62.

[21] Dom Thomas Verner Moore, *The Driving Forces of Human Nature and Their Adjustment* (New York: Grune & Stratton, 1950).

[22] Alfred Adler, *Studie über Minderwertigkeit von Organen* (Berlin-Vienna, 1907), p. 92.

[23] William C. Kvaraceus, *et al.*, *Review of Educational Research*, XXIX (Washington, D.C.: American Educational Research Association, 1959), p. 423.

[24] Frank T. Wilson, "Working with the Motives of Gifted Children," *Elementary School Journal*, LVII (February, 1957), pp. 247-52.

[25] Strang, *loc. cit.*, p. 302.

[26] Ernest R. Hilgard, *Theories of Learning* (New York: Appleton-Century-Crofts, Inc., 1956).

[27] John C. Gowan, "The Underachieving Gifted Child—A Problem for Everyone," *Exceptional Children*, XXI (April, 1955), pp. 247-49, 270-71.

[28] *Ibid.*, p. 248.

[29] David B. Orr, "Opportunities for Research on the Education of Gifted Students," *The Gifted Student*, Co-operative Research Monograph (Washington, D.C.: U.S. Government Printing Office, 1960), p. 67.

[30] Rev. Russell R. Novello, "The Self-Concept and Its Measurement," (Washington, D.C.: U.S. Government Printing Office, 1960).

[31] Strang, *loc. cit.*, p. 458.

[32] Robert F. DeHaan and Robert J. Havighurst, *Educating Gifted Children* (Chicago: University of Chicago Press, 1957), p. 6.

[33] *Ibid.*, p. 102.

[34] *Ibid.*, p. 103.

[35] Norma Cutts and Nicholas Moseley, *Bright Children: A Guide for Parents* (New York: G. P. Putnam's Sons, 1953).

[36] Morris Krugman and Irene H. Impellizzeri, "Identification and Guidance of Underachieving Gifted Students in New York City," *Exceptional Children*, XXVI (February, 1960), p. 283.

Appendix

FRANCIS J. CONNELL, C.SS.R., S.T.D., LL.D., L.H.D.

The Mixed-Marriage Promises

▶▶

The Catholic Church has always been opposed to mixed marriages—that is, marriages between Catholics and persons of other religious beliefs or of no religious belief. The Code of Canon Law, the official compilation of Church legislation, definitely states that the Church "everywhere most severely prohibits mixed marriages" (Canon 1066). In making this law the Church is actually promoting the welfare of non-Catholics as well as of Catholics, for statistics prove that the proportion of marriages that turn out unhappily is greater when the parties are of different religious belief than when both profess the same religion. Hence, in forbidding mixed marriages the Church is helping to diminish the number of unhappy homes.

Fundamentally, however, the Church's opposition to mixed marriages is based on the doctrine that there is only one true religion. The Church will never cease to teach and Catholics will never cease to believe that Jesus Christ, the Son of God, established only one church and imposed on all men the obligation to be members of that Church. That one true and authorized church is the Catholic Church. Of course, this does not mean that only Catholics can possess the grace of God and be saved. On the contrary, there are many non-Catholics who are striving in accordance with the dictates of an honest conscience to live good lives and love God with their whole heart and soul. These good persons are actually connected with the Catholic Church by implicit desire (since they wish to do God's will and it is God's will that they join the Catholic Church), and if they die with these dispositions, they will be saved.

Nevertheless, even for such persons it is a great misfortune not to be members of the one true Church. As Pope Pius XII said, speaking of sincere non-Catholics: "Even though unsuspectingly they are related to the Mystical Body of the Redeemer in desire and resolution, they still remain deprived of so many precious gifts and helps from heaven, which one can enjoy only in the Catholic Church" (*Mystici corporis*, n. 100).

Since God wills all human beings to be members of the Catholic Church, Catholic parents have a grave obligation to have all their children baptized and brought up as Catholics. For parents have the first responsibility for the spiritual, as well as the bodily welfare of their offspring. In other words, a Catholic would be guilty of a mortal sin if he brought a child into the world without the firm intention of having him baptized and reared in the Catholic Church. Moreover, the Church commands that Catholics have their children baptized *as soon as possible* after birth (Canon 770), which, according to the common interpretation of theologians, means within a month, at the most.

Now, when a Catholic marries a non-Catholic he is likely to put himself in danger of losing his Catholic faith or of becoming lax in its practice. Married persons, living together in close association year after year, exert a great influence on each other. Furthermore, the Catholic who marries a non-Catholic creates a situation that is likely to be dangerous to the faith of the children who may be born of the union. Perhaps the non-Catholic is very fervent in the practice of his particular religion, and naturally he would like to see his sons and daughters join his own church, and perhaps will openly manifest this desire. Or, on the other hand, he may be very careless in the practice of religion, never going to church, never saying a prayer. This, too, can bring about a dangerous situation, the probability that the children will be influenced by their non-Catholic parent to become indifferent to religion.

Consequently, a Catholic may not enter marriage with a non-Catholic as long as there is grave danger to his own faith or to the faith of the offspring. We say "grave" danger because a mixed marriage always involves some spiritual risk. But if the grave danger is removed and only a light risk remains, this can be tolerated if there is a good reason for the marriage. It must be noted that we are concerned now with the law of God from which the Church cannot dispense. In the words of the Code of Canon Law: "If there is danger of the perversion (loss of faith) of the Catholic party and of the children, the marriage is forbidden even by divine law" (Canon 1060).

The Church has added its own prohibition of mixed

marriages to the prohibition of divine law. However, for sufficient reasons the Church can give a dispensation from its own legislation. But this does not mean that the marriage is by that very fact rendered lawful. The divine law must still be taken into account, which means that the grave danger to the faith of the Catholic party and of the children must be removed. Only then will the marriage cease to be opposed to the law of God. In extraordinary cases the danger could be removed without formal promises on the part of the couple—for example, if both are so advanced in years that there certainly will be no children and the Catholic party is so staunch in the faith that he surely will not be spiritually harmed by the marriage. But ordinarily, adequate assurance that there will be no danger to the faith of the Catholic or of the children cannot be obtained unless the non-Catholic promises that he will not interfere with the religion of the Catholic spouse and both promise that all the children will be baptized and brought up as Catholics. The Church will never give a dispensation for a mixed marriage unless these conditions are fulfilled. Moreover, there must be reasonable certainty that the couple will live up to these agreements.

Although in certain circumstances verbal promises would suffice, the Church ordinarily requires the promises to be made in writing. Indeed, this is the customary procedure in the case of any important agreement. Unfortunately, there are many persons who will readily deny unrecorded statements. This they cannot do when documents can be produced to which they have affixed their signature.

Such is the explanation of the promises that the Church requires from the persons who are about to contract a mixed marriage. At the present day there is considerable objection to these promises on the part of non-Catholics, and sometimes even on the part of Catholics. We are told that there can be no "ecumenical approach" toward Protestants unless we eliminate the promises and leave the matter of the religion of the Catholic spouse and of the children entirely to the conscience of the parties themselves. Such a statement is supposed to have been made by Fr. Hans Küng, a priest from Germany who has been lecturing in the United States. When Catholics read such statements they should realize that even priests can make mistakes. It is astounding to think that a Catholic, believing that there is only one true Church and that it is supremely important to belong to that Church, could say that a Catholic may lawfully marry a non-Catholic without making certain that he or she will not suffer loss of faith and that all the children will be baptized and brought up as Catholics. To reject a principle that the Church has taught for centuries merely to please non-Catholics is false ecumenism.

Sometimes the objection is heard that it is not fair for the Church to demand that *all* the children be brought up as Catholics. Why not allow an arrangement whereby the boys will be brought up in the religion of the father and the girls in the religion of the mother? The blunt answer is that truth admits of no compromise. If one person holds that two plus two makes six and another holds that the sum is four, can this latter agree that they compromise and say that the answer is five? Of course, not. He must continue to hold that two plus two makes four, for he knows it is the only correct answer. Similarly, the Catholic

Church cannot compromise on a single point of its teaching. The Church knows that she has been commissioned by Jesus Christ to preach His doctrine without modification and to bring as many as possible to the acceptance of the one true religion. Hence, there can be no "50-50 deal" as far as Catholic doctrine is concerned. If the Church gave approval for a single child to be brought up as a non-Catholic, she would not be functioning as the true Church and she would be guilty of gross disloyalty to her Divine Founder.

But did not the Church at one period of her history allow mixed marriages to be contracted with the agreement that the boys would follow the religion of the father and the girls that of the mother? It is true, instances of this kind did take place in the early part of the nineteenth century, some in Germany and some even in the United States. The famous Chief Justice Taney, the first Catholic to hold this high office in our land, married a Protestant lady in the presence of a priest with this agreement concerning the children (he subsequently had six daughters and no sons). But such instances only prove that there were some priests (and perhaps even some bishops) who were ignorant or neglectful of their duty. This arrangement was never sanctioned by the Popes, but on the contrary was condemned by them. Thus in 1830 Pope Pius VIII wrote to the bishops of Prussia: "It is known that Catholics, whether men or women, who contract marriage with non-Catholics in such wise as to expose themselves or their future offspring to the danger of perversion not only violate the canon law but also directly and most gravely sin against the natural and the divine law" (Gasparri, *Fontes*, p. 734).

An excuse for the refusal on the part of the non-Catholic to fulfill his promises sometimes takes the form of a statement that he was *forced* by the Church to make these promises and therefore is not bound to live up to them, since it is a principle of justice that a person is not bound to a contract if he was coerced into making it. But this is a very shallow excuse. The Church never forces a non-Catholic to make the promises. On the contrary, he is in a sense forcing the Church to allow him to marry a Catholic, and the Church is reluctantly granting permission, at the same time laying down a condition that she is obliged to impose by the law of God. The Church would prefer that he would refuse to make the promises; and if any non-Catholic feels that he is not allowed full freedom in making the promises, he should have the honesty to declare this. Of course, in such a case the Church would not grant a dispensation for the mixed marriage, but that would undoubtedly turn out for the better interests of both parties. Actually, most Protestant ministers, if they have had much experience in the ministry, are just as earnest in telling their people not to marry Catholics as Catholic priests are in telling their people not to marry non-Catholics.

It might be asked if the Church has any regard for the conscience of the non-Catholic party of a mixed marriage when she requires him to promise that all the children will be baptized and brought up as Catholics. The answer is that many non-Catholics have no qualms of conscience in making the promises, since they regard all religions as equally good. Others doubtless regard the Catholic religion as false, and such persons are violating the dictates of their conscience if they make the promises. The Catholic Church respects the sincerity of such persons and urges them not to make the promises, since they would thereby commit a subjective sin. But such persons should give up the idea of marrying a Catholic, because the Church will not grant them a dispensation.

The Code of Canon Law also declares that the Catholic party of a mixed marriage is bound to strive prudently for the conversion of the non-Catholic (Canon 1062). By the general law of the Church, however, the Catholic is not bound to give a signed promise to this effect, though this may be required by certain bishops. But here too we have another prescription of divine law. In Christian charity every Catholic is bound in accordance with his particular situation in life, to induce non-Catholics to study Catholic teaching. He should make a special effort in regard to those who are near and dear to him, as is certainly the case with a husband or wife. Needless to say, this effort should be prudent and charitable. No coercion or immoderate petitions may be employed. Indeed, the Church will not admit anyone to its membership unless that person is intellectually convinced that the Catholic religion is the one true faith. In any event, the Catholic party has always available two good means of helping the non-Catholic to perceive the truth of the Catholic faith—prayer for his conversion and good example.

There are some persons today—including even some Catholics—who would like to see the Church do away with the law requiring the presence of a priest for the *validity* of a mixed marriage. This would mean that though the couple went before a non-Catholic minister or a civil official, they would contract a true marriage just as if they appeared before a priest. The Church could indeed make such a change, because it is only by ecclesiastical legislation that two Catholics or a Catholic and a non-Catholic must appear before a priest and two witnesses in order to contract a valid marriage. However, even if such a modification of the law were made, it should be emphasized that a Catholic would be guilty of the sin of participating in forbidden worship if he appeared before a non-Catholic clergyman. Furthermore, the Catholic party would still have the obligation of bringing up all the children in the Catholic faith. The Church could not dispense with this condition, because it is a precept of divine law.

It should be remembered, also, that in addition to the promises, the Church demands that there be good reasons for a mixed marriage. For, there is always some danger to the faith (of the Catholic party and of the future offspring) in a mixed marriage, so good reasons are required to offset this danger and to justify the Catholic in running the risk. Thus, if there is a solid reason to believe that the non-Catholic party will enter the Church, there is a good reason for the marriage. Again, if a Catholic widow with several children to support receives a proposal of marriage from an honorable Protestant gentleman who will undoubtedly live up to the promises, she has an adequate reason for entering marriage with him. But the mere fact that the young couple love each other ardently is not a sufficient reason. Sometimes, indeed, the Church grants a dispensation through fear that otherwise the couple will go through a marriage ceremony before a civil official or a non-Catholic minister; but, as is quite evident, such a reason implies a bad disposition on the part of the Catholic.

Some mixed marriages turn out very happily, and when such a case occurs, the parties involved should be grateful to God. But unfortunately, others lead to conflict, carelessness in religion, and even loss of faith, particularly on the part of the children. The Church cannot be indifferent to such unquestionable facts. The Church is the Mystical Body of Jesus Christ, and just as the living physical body takes care to protect its members from physical harm, so the Church, under the guidance of its Head, Jesus Christ, strives to guard its members from situations that may harm them spiritually. Among such perilous situations mixed marriages take a prominent place.

The practical conclusion is that Catholics should not choose persons of other religious beliefs (or of no belief) to be their life-partners. Young Catholics should avoid "steady dating" with non-Catholics, however attractive they may be. When a boy and a girl love each other very much, they see only the good qualities of the other. Difference of religion does not seem to be a very important obstacle to marriage. But after they have been married several years, disagreements and conflicts on the matter of religion may arise and become a source of serious unhappiness in the home. Hence, we can see the wisdom of the advice that the Church is constantly repeating to her children: "Marry your own."

The Morality of Prize Fighting

▶▶

In January 1950 I answered a question in *The American Ecclesiastical Review* regarding the morality of prize fighting and boxing. These two terms are sometimes used synonymously, but I made a definite distinction. Boxing, as I explained it, means the parrying of light blows, as a contest of skill and speed, without any intention of striking the adversary severely or inflicting injury. This type of sport, I asserted, is perfectly lawful as a means of exercise and recreation, and a lawful way to train a person in self-defense. But, I continued, prize fighting consists in striking the opponent as hard as one can and, if possible, inflicting a "knock out." This I claimed is unlawful, as a violation of the fifth commandment (*The American Ecclesiastical Review*, CXXII, 1 [Jan. 1950], 58).

In *Catholic Men* for February, 1951, I developed this theme more fully. I said: "Does God's law permit a person to rain blows with all his strength on a fellow man in the endeavor to hurt him, and even to render him incapable of continuing the contest? The answer would seem to be that this is a violation of the fifth commandment of God."

Other articles in agreement with my view appeared in this same periodical in December, 1953, and in October, 1957. Let me add that I was not the first to claim that prize fighting is immoral. For many years before his death Fr. James Gillis, C.S.P., vigorously opposed professional fighting. But I believe that my statements have brought the matter to the fore, coupled with the fact that in recent years there have been more tragic incidents than previously in the ring, which have induced the public to consider seriously the morality of this form of sport.

I believe I can say without hesitation that in the course of the past twelve years the majority of those who have written on this subject have condemned prize fighting. My opinion has received the valued support of Father G. Kelly, S.J., in *Theological Studies*, XII (1951), 78. In *MacClean's Magazine* for January 15, 1950, Ray Gardner, a former sports editor, wrote: "The sport dignified by the name boxing is no sport at all, but in its worst aspects is a vicious, man-destroying racket. It is a racket that often seduces clean-cut, healthy kids with the promise of glory and easy money, squeezes blood-money out of them, and then callously tosses them aside, broken physically, mentally and morally."

America for November 18, 1950, carried an article by Timothy A. Murnane, who approved the stand I had taken. The writer quotes a view expressed by the late Father E. Healy, S.J., who said in his *Moral Guidance* that "the knock out ordinarily does not do the victim much harm." Mr. Murnane, while disagreeing with Father Healy, excuses his statement on the ground that he was not familiar with the more recent studies about the harm that is done by a knock out, especially when it is repeated a number of times. Mr. Murnane concludes with a quotation from a sportswriter, Dan Ryan: "We simply need a new sanity code in boxing. Both God's law and man's reason point to the urgent necessity of a reform in present boxing regulations."

In 1952 an excellent doctoral dissertation on *The Morality of Prize Fighting*, by the Rev. George Bernard, C.S.C., was published by the School of Theology of the Catholic University of America. The author goes into great detail in his description of the bodily injury that prize fighting can cause, particularly to the brain. Speaking of the suggestion that many accidents and deaths will be avoided if the fighters wear a head protector, Father Bernard remarks: "This piece of equipment has been employed for some time in collegiate matches as well as in the training quarters of most professional boxers. It offers some assurance against cuts around the eyes, and it gives some protection to the skull in case of falls, but there is doubt whether or not it protects the brain against injury. It would seem that a jolt to the head would cause the brain to oscillate, even though the head is covered by a leather helmet" (p. 103).

In 1952 the *Journal of the American Medical Association* in an editorial called for an all-out effort—including a redesigning of boxing gloves—to cut the high incidence of deaths and injuries in the ring. The editorial stated that in the years 1946-52 eighty-seven prize fighters are known to have died throughout the world of injuries sustained in the ring, forty-seven of them in the United States.

In 1955 Judge Eliah Adlow of Massachusetts gave a

statement in connection with the death from prize fighting of a certain Ed Sonders, containing these words: "We cannot ignore the obvious fact that the safety and the welfare of the participants have been subordinated to the spectators' lust for brutality" (Boston *Herald*, Jan. 15, 1955).

The *Linacre Quarterly* for May 1958 carried an article by Dr. E. G. Laforet, on "Boxing, Medicine and Morals" in which the question is discussed mainly from the medical standpoint, and the conclusion is drawn that "the medical evidence which indicates that boxing is always potentially dangerous to life, and often actually so, lends strong support to this view (that prize fighting is morally wrong)."

In the *Saturday Evening Post* for October 25, 1958, there appeared an article by Harold Barnes, a veteran ringside official, under the heading "Let's Abolish Boxing." He said: "I consider boxing legalized murder" and went on to speak of the "many former fighters who are walking the streets on wobbly legs, their minds not so sharp as before they started fighting, their reason, memory, self-control and coordination all impaired by repeated head blows. Possibly as many as five out of 100 become completely punch-drunk and wind up in mental institutions."

In England in 1952 a complete abolition of both amateur and professional boxing was advocated on both medical and moral grounds by Dr. Edith Summerskill, a member of Parliament and a physician. The newspaper account of the controversy stated, however, that her attempt would probably fail, since "boxing is growing in popularity throughout the country, and professional fights are regularly televised. . . . Those who disagree with Dr. Summerskill say that fewer deaths or permanent injuries result from boxing than from many other sports. Others insist that the discipline of boxing builds self-control and character" (*New York Times*, Jan. 26, 1952).

Many other quotations could be given, but I believe the above references adequately show that there has been during the last decade a strong movement to abolish prize fighting as it actually exists, especially in the United States. Now, in 1962, this movement has become much stronger, particularly because of the death of a young fighter in a championship match, viewed by millions on television. Many writers in the secular press have made this the occasion of a vehement denunciation of prize fighting in general and have called for the abolition or at least the modification of the procedures employed in this "sport." An editorial in the *New York Times* asks: "This is the Saturday night pleasure of a civilized people? This is a game that we recognize as an approved form of athletics, to be governed by a commission under state auspices as a manly entertainment? This is an 'exhibition' for those too kindly, too humane to endure the bestial savagery of the bullfight?"

The London *Daily Sketch* called the bout which resulted in the death of Paret "the most murderous world title fight in history." The New York *Post* called prize fighting "organized primitivism" and demanded that it be outlawed. The Vatican radio declared "Professional boxing is a morally objectionable sport."

It is time for Catholic priests, as exponents of the moral law, to consider seriously the morality of prize fighting. In view of the widespread denunciation of this form of amusement, and medical and moral arguments against it, it is difficult to see how anyone who follows Christian principles can uphold it as lawful. One of the most frequent arguments for the lawfulness of prize fighting is the statement that there are more injuries and even deaths in some other sports, such as football, than occur in the ring. But the answer is evident. First, many more persons engage in those other games than in the "fight game." Second, the primary purpose of prize fighting is to injure the opponent, though not necessarily permanently. Each contestant punches the other as vehemently as he can; and certainly, this is a violation of the fifth commandment, as the Catholic Church interprets it. An article on prize fighting in *Time* for April 13, 1962, entitled "The Aim is to Maim" says that when a fighter in the ring hits his opponent on the head his objective is to render him temporarily unconscious. Bodily injury that occurs in other sports occurs only *per accidens*, not by direct intention. The argument was thus proposed by Fr. Bernard in his dissertation mentioned above:

> It is not lawful to do a person direct bodily harm except by way of punishment in the cause of justice. But prize fighters cause immoderate bodily harm to their opponents by the blows which they voluntarily strike, nor is the harm done by way of punishment nor with proper authority. Therefore, prize fighters act unlawfully. But since the participants of prize fighting are "playing" according to the rules of the "game,"—points are awarded for forceful hits *in proportion to their damaging effect*— then the "game" itself is immoral (p. 143).

It has been suggested that the use of headgear and of larger gloves might make prize fighting morally permissible. It is true, such measures might diminish the risk of serious injury, but I doubt if they would free prize fighting from the guilt of sin. The fighters would still strike each other as hard as possible, and I am sure that there would be real injury inflicted. In other words, the motive and the results would still be substantially the same as they are at present.

Another deplorable feature in prize fighting is the effect on the spectators. Fr. Bernard describes the feature as follows:

> The crowd comes to the fights expecting and wanting to see knock outs. It is like the home run in baseball. If their desires are not fulfilled, they often taunt the fighters to induce them to put a little more power into their blows. Often too the excitement engendered by the combat they are witnessing causes many of the spectators to lose control of themselves. The blood becomes heated and the emotions overrule reason; base, animal instincts prevail (p. 27).

Another undesirable feature of prize fighting apparently is the dishonesty it may involve. Since I have no direct evidence of this I can only say that the fighters, promotors, managers and gamblers are said at times to use dishonest methods in order to make money on a fight. If this be true, it is another argument against professional prize fighting.

I believe that in view of all that has been said, priests should try to have professional prize fighting abolished in the United States. In this should be included also the Golden Gloves tournaments, for these too, whatever they may be called, are fights, aimed at scoring a knock out. I believe that priests should not foster boxing bouts in their social centers, for again these are, or at least they lead to, fighting. If our people ask us about the morality of prize fights, I believe they should be told that these are morally wrong, for I cannot see any probability to the contrary.

In this way we can show the world that the Catholic Church has moral standards that pave the way to a more practical manifestation of the great commandment: "Thou shalt love thy neighbor as thyself."

The Morality of Juvenile Courtships

▶▶

In present-day America the conduct of adolescents, or "teenagers," is deservedly an object of much concern. It must be admitted truthfully and humbly that up to the present the efforts to check juvenile delinquency have been far from successful, and that the situation is becoming worse. A recent survey of juvenile delinquency under the direction of a subcommittee of the United States Senate has revealed the appalling fact that there has been an increase of 45 per cent in law infractions on the part of youngsters in the past five years.[1] In view of such findings we can heartily agree with the forthright statement of Archbishop Cushing of Boston, contained in his New Year's radio message: "America's most humiliating failure during 1954 was its inability to cope with the growing generation." [2]

One of the contributory causes toward juvenile delinquency is the custom of "going steady"—the frequent and exclusive association of a boy and girl in their early teens. I am not concerned here with company-keeping by a couple who can reasonably look forward to marriage within a reasonable period of time, even though they may be teen-agers. Thus, a girl of seventeen in her senior high school year may be keeping steady company with a youth of nineteen, who plans to marry her within a year following her graduation. Such a marriage may be imprudent because of the immaturity of the couple, but in itself it would not be contrary to divine or ecclesiastical legislation. Indeed, such early marriages may sometimes prove ideal. Hence, steady company-keeping by such a youthful couple is not in itself objectionable, though the rules laid down in our standard works of Moral Theology for *procationes*, as their meetings are called, must be observed for the protection of chastity.[3]

The topic I am discussing is the steady company-keeping of a young boy and a girl, usually between the ages of twelve and fifteen, who have no idea of marrying and could not reasonably marry, even if they wished, for at least five or six years. This form of association has become quite common in our country in recent years. According to Dr. Paul Landis, Professor of Sociology at Washington State College, "one nationwide poll of thousands of high school teen-agers showed that the majority thought they should be allowed to go steady."[4]

Steady company-keeping by adolescents would not in itself be regarded as an instance of juvenile delinquency by most sociologists and police officials, who restrict this expression to such wrongdoing as drunkenness, drug addiction and crimes of violence. But those who accept the interpretation of the sixth commandment proposed by the Catholic Church would agree that in many cases of juvenile company-keeping serious sins against God's law are committed. It is a well-established fact that in many juvenile circles the indecent practice known as "petting" is regarded as a normal procedure between a boy and a girl who date each other frequently. In the words of Dr. Landis: "After young people have begun to date, it is expected that there will be some display of affection." [5] The June 14, 1954 edition of *Life* carried an article on juvenile company-keeping, with pictures quite frankly representing the ardent love-making of a youthful pair, the impression being given that this is the ordinary concomitant of steady company-keeping. With such a situation so prevalent in our land, it is not surprising to read the statement of Dr. Goodrich Schauffler of Portland, Oregon, made at a recent Congress on Obstetrics and Gynecology, to the effect that in the past fifteen years illegitimate births among teen-age girls have doubled in number. [6]

How should the priest meet this social and moral problem? In the first place he must not be led astray by the way in which the world regards juvenile company-keeping. The moral perils of this practice, formerly recognized by all intelligent and decent persons, non-Catholic as well as Catholic, are utterly overlooked by many today, even though some of them may frown on it for other reasons. Thus, Isabella Taves, described as a "nationally known writer on teen-age problems," concludes a study of this subject with the statement: "I don't think going steady [by young teen-agers] is a good idea," but the moral dangers of the practice seem to have little weight toward this conclusion, and she views the greatest danger as the emphasis it puts on fidelity too early in life. [7]

Even some Catholic writers seem to underestimate the

moral risks of steady company-keeping, as long as no sin has actually occurred. Thus, a widely used manual of religious instruction contains the statement that steady company-keeping is neither harmful nor sinful "as long as the companionship is kept within bounds," which phrase means, I presume, "as long as the couple have not sinned." This is certainly too lenient a decision, if one accepts the commonly accepted Catholic doctrine about frequenting the occasions of sin. No priest, familiar with the approved theological teaching on the matter of company-keeping, should allow himself to view this problem so lightly.

Neither should a priest become so pessimistic about the situation as to believe that nothing can be done about it. That is not the way in which the Catholic Church treats abuses. If a sinful custom prevails, those who have the care of the flock of Christ are supposed to attempt to eradicate it, even though it has taken a strong hold and the first efforts seem to bear little fruit. A very definite stand on this matter has been taken by the Bishops of Canada, who recently made this statement:

> We call upon parents to discourage and extirpate, as far as lies in their power, the pernicious custom of boys and girls in their early teens forming permanent and ex-clusive "steady" associations which are so often an occasion of sin. Heavy indeed will be the reckoning of parents who from negligence or fear of displeasing their children or from a desire to appear "modern" allow their children the freedom which common sense rejects as premature.[8]

Our textbooks of Moral Theology, discussing the subject under the heading of *procatio* or *nupturientes*, teach that steady company-keeping in itself is an occasion of sin; however, the hope of marriage in the near future will justify it, as long as the proper safeguards are observed.[9]

But what is required to constitute the association of a boy and girl steady company-keeping? It is not easy to define the term exactly, despite the fact that it is frequently employed in daily conversation. Isabella Taves defines it in a rather sophisticated manner as "an agreement between a girl and boy, usually in their early teens, to date only each other—without benefit of ring, fraternity pin, specific intentions or (and here's the rub) telling their parents." [10] I would take exception to this last phrase, because many parents know and approve the steady company-keeping of their children. To form a definition that will help toward a theological solution of this problem, I suggest that the following factors combined may be regarded as constituting steady company-keeping:

(1) The association of the two must be *frequent*. A boy and girl who go out with each other only once or twice a month can hardly be said to be keeping company, at least if they have the opportunity to meet more frequently. However, the amount of time they spend together would have to be taken into consideration. A pair who meet only once a week but spend three or four hours together could be regarded as company-keepers more correctly than a boy and girl who meet two or three times a week in the drug-store for a coke and a talk of a half-hour's duration. But certainly a couple who spend two or three evenings a week together fulfill this condition of company-keeping.

(2) The association must be *exclusive*—that is, there must be an understanding that she is his "girl-friend" and he is her "boy-friend." Of course, an occasional date of each

with another juvenile would not nullify this condition. From a questionnaire sent out by Fr. James P. Conroy, Associate Editor of *Our Sunday Visitor*, we learn that 53 per cent of the young folks asked—almost 25,000 in number—defined steady dating as dating *mainly* with one person. From this same survey it is also evident that it is customary for those who are going steady to signify the fact in such a way that all others may see it, by the exchange of class rings, pins, braceltes, etc., as well as by the fact that the two are seen together at dances, movies, etc. An ordinary feature of this exclusiveness is that they pass some time in places in which they cannot be seen by others. As is evident, this is the most dangerous aspect of steady company-keeping.

(3) The association must be motivated by *some measure of affection*. It is possible that mere expediency or convenience may be the only reason for their company-keeping. Thus, if a boy and a girl happen to be the only Catholic juveniles in a small community, they might go to school together and return together and meet two or three times a week in each other's home to go over the school-work, with a feeling of friendliness, but without any of the emotional attitude designated as love or affection. Their motive of exclusive association might be the fact that they feel it safer for Catholic adolescents to associate with one another rather than with non-Catholics, or the fact that they are convinced that there is less moral danger with each other than with the other boys and girls of the community. Indeed, some of the adolescents who answered Father Conroy's questionnaire mentioned as a motive for steady company-keeping the unwillingness to take chances with a

person whose moral standards are not clearly known. I do not believe that it happens often that a boy and a girl associate with each other frequently and exclusively without developing affection. Nevertheless, if this factor is lacking, and they regard each other merely as good friends, they cannot be said to be in the category of steady company-keepers.

It does not follow that if any of these three conditions is not present a boy and a girl can be permitted to associate with each other as often as they choose or under any circumstances they may select. Even a type of association that is not steady company-keeping in the strict sense may be a proximate occasion of sin for a particular couple. Thus, a boy and girl may go out with each other only once or twice a month, but if they commit sin on these occasions, their meetings must be discontinued, or at least definite precautions must be taken to avoid relapse.

If, however, these three conditions are verified, the couple can be said to be keeping steady company, and the rules accepted by theologians for such a case are to be followed by the confessor. Now, it is the common theological opinion that a couple who put themselves in such circumstances are in an occasion of sin, and consequently are doing wrong by frequenting such an occasion unless they have a sufficient justifying reason. But, the only reason proposed by theologians as justifying steady company-keeping is the expectation (with at least some probability) of marriage in the near future. Thus, Noldin-Schmitt assert: "The hope of a future marriage is the only reason why these visits are rendered licit." [11] In the cases we are considering there is surely no hope of marriage, at least within a reasonable time. Some might claim that the assurance of having a date for social functions would constitute a justifying reason, but with this I cannot agree. At any rate, the mere fact that "everybody is doing it" or the fear of being ridiculed as being unable to attract adolescents of the opposite sex does not constitute a sufficient reason.

From this it follows that adolescent company-keeping in the conditions described is sinful because the young couple are putting themselves in the occasion of grave sin without a sufficient reason. Does it follow necessarily that they are always in a *proximate* occasion of grave sin and consequently guilty of *grave* sin? I would hesitate to state this as a universal conclusion, though I would agree with the statement of Father Damen, that company-keeping is *generally* a proximate occasion of grave sin (and consequently forbidden *sub gravi*) when it is practiced without any intention of entering marriage or when there is no hope of marriage in the near future.[12]

In any event, if a boy and a girl have proved that this manner of association is a proximate occasion of sin for them, they are guilty of mortal sin by continuing this type of companionship without any expectation of marriage in the near future. The fact that they have committed grave sin together is a sufficient proof that their steady company-keeping is a proximate occasion of grave sin, and hence must be given up. In the words of Wouters: "As soon as the company-keepers have sinned gravely, the occasion has become proximate, and must be treated as such by the confessor." [13]

The accepted theological doctrine on this matter is thus

expressed by Noldin-Schmitt: "When boys and girls accuse themselves of external sins against chastity with a person of the other sex, they are to be asked if they are keeping company with this person. If they answer in the affirmative, they are to be asked further if there is any hope of a future marriage. If there is no such hope, and if, *a fortiori*, there is no intention of matrimony, it is absolutely necessary that they break off the company-keeping, since they are in a proximate occasion of grave sin without a just cause." [14] This statement gives the confessor a norm to be followed when a young person, with no hope of marriage (at least within a reasonable time), accuses himself or herself of sinning gravely with a "steady." The company-keeping must be stopped, and if the penitent will not promise to follow this procedure, absolution must be denied. At most, a date in the future could be permitted on rare occasions on condition that they are not alone at any time.

But what of the adolescent who is keeping steady company, but sincerely asserts that there has been no violation of chastity with his companion? From the fact that nothing sinful has yet occurred it does not necessarily follow that the two are not in any proximate danger of grave sin. The confessor may prudently judge from the character of the penitent or from other circumstances—for example, the fact that a boy previously associated with particular girl friends and ended by sinning with them—that there is a truly proximate danger of grave sin in this companionship. In that event, he must forbid the company-keeping, and must deny absolution if this condition is not accepted.

It should be noted also that a youth's statement that

there has been no grave sin in his meetings with his "steady" is not always to be taken at its face value. Some modern adolescents have strange ideas about the morality of love-making, regarding only a consummating sexual act as a grave sin. Hence, the boy who assures the confessor that there has been nothing of a sinful nature between himself and his girl-friend may be found, on closer questioning, to be indulging with her in passionate kisses and embraces, in accordance with the methods used in the movies, apparently without realizing that their companionship has reached (at least objectively) a stage of mortal sin.

Furthermore, when the confessor meets a case of apparently innocent company-keeping, an important factor is the religious affiliation of the other party. This is particularly the case when there is any probability—as there sometimes is—that eventually (after several years) the two may marry. If it is found out that the other party is a non-Catholic, such a courtship must be terminated at once, unless there are (or at least will be at the time of the marriage) grave and lawful reasons for contracting it.[15]

However, what is to be done in the case when the steady company-keeping has been perfectly chaste between a Catholic boy and a Catholic girl and there is no reason to fear that it is for them a proximate occasion of sin? It should be remembered that even in this case, when there is no hope for a marriage within a reasonable period of time, the company-keeping must be reckoned a venial sin, inasmuch as the couple are frequenting a remote occasion of grave sin without a sufficient reason.[16] Furthermore, such steady company-keeping helps to promote a custom that is surely dangerous to the younger generation in general. However, if a priest can persuade himself honestly that in a particular case the young persons are not committing mortal sin by their steady company-keeping he could give absolution, even though the company-keeping will be continued. He should, however, urge that it be discontinued. And the words of St. Alphonsus should be noted: "Generally speaking, in regard to boys and girls who love each other, although they are not all to be charged indiscriminately with mortal sin, ordinarily I believe they find it difficult to be outside the proximate occasion of sinning gravely. This is more than evident from experience; for out of a hundred youths hardly two or three in this occasion will be found free from mortal sins." [17]

The priest's zeal in eradicating this modern abuse should not be confined to the confessional. In sermons and conferences to young folks, especially on the occasion of retreats, junior Holy Name gatherings, sodality meetings, etc., the topic of juvenile company-keeping should be discussed, and it should be pointed out that this custom is reprehensible because it frequently involves loss of time and neglect of study, because it eliminates the normal joys of adolescence, and especially because it involves moral dangers. It should be explained that the association of boys and girls in a group at parties, etc., is permissible provided they meet each other in the manner proper to decent Catholic boys and girls. But care should be taken that at any social affairs under Church auspices there should be nothing that is morally reprehensible, such as cheek-to-cheek dancing, dimmed lights, etc.

In our Catholic high schools both principals and teachers, as well as the priests having administrative posts, should instruct the pupils on the proper attitude to maintain toward this growing evil of steady company-keeping by juveniles who have no hope of marriage in the near future. There can be occasions in which severe disciplinary measures may have to be taken toward some pupils who are known to be indulging in too free associations with members of the other sex. At times even expulsion from school should not be regarded as too severe a measure in the case of refractory boys or girls.

Above all, priests should endeavor to persuade Catholic parents to fulfill their obligation to direct and guide their sons and daughters according to the law of God. From the survey made by Father Conroy it appears that 46 per cent of the parents of juvenile company-keepers are either favorable or indifferent toward this custom of their sons and daughters. Some parents think it "cute" when children of thirteen or fourteen become enamored with each other: and some are thrilled when a little boy falls in love with their little daughter who would normally be finding her recreation with adolescents of her own sex. A return to the traditional way of domestic life would be greatly beneficial in modern society, and Catholic parents should lead the way by giving their children a home life that is happy and holy. If parents themselves set loose standards, what can we expect of their offspring? As the authors of the articles in the *Saturday Evening Post* remark, we should not be shocked by the revelation of sexual promiscuity among high-school students, when adults make a big business of glamorizing sex.[18]

This matter has graver implications than the particular

subject of juvenile company-keeping. Beyond doubt, one of the reasons why our young Catholics are keeping steady company is the conviction that "everyone else is doing it." Catholics must be warned against the attitude that they can base their conduct on the ways of the world. They must be taught from childhood that if they wish to live up to the principles of their faith they must be willing to be different from non-Catholics and must be willing to be ridiculed as old-fashioned. And, they must know this is the way to bring to the attention of the world the true standards of morality. In the words of Archbishop Noll: "If teen-age Catholics have any duty it is to lead others who have never had any special moral training and not to follow others. Every one instructed in the knowledge of God is obligated to be a leader, and may not follow one who is not so instructed." [19]

Priests must direct the laity along this way, by word and especially by example. Priests are men who have chosen a way of life very different from that of people of the world because it exemplifies in a high degree the ideals of the Christian life laid down by Our Lord Himself; hence, they must be models of virtue for their people. Catholic men and women—and even children—must learn that it is not easy to be a good Catholic, and that they must be prepared to face scorn and hatred and ridicule if they would be accounted faithful followers of Jesus Christ.

NOTES

[1] R. Clendenen and H. Beaser, "The Shame of America," *Saturday Evening Post,* Jan. 8, 1955, p. 17.

[2] NCWC News Release, Jan. 3, 1955.

[3] Cf. Aertnys-Damen, *Theologia moralis* (Turin, 1950), II, n. 517-24; Noldin-Schmitt, *Summa theologiae moralis* (Innsbruch, 1954), III, 419-20; Iorio, *Theologia moralis* (Naples, 1947), III, 885-89; Jone, *Moral Theology* (Westminster, Md., 1951), nn. 240, 607.

[4] Landis, Paul H., "Should Teen-agers Go Steady?" *World Telegram and Sun Saturday Magazine*, Jan. 8, 1955, p. 4.

[5] *Ibid.*

[6] *Newsweek*, Dec. 27, 1954, p. 49.

[7] Taves, Isabella, "Should Young Teeners go Steady?" *The American Weekly*, April 18, 1954, p. 7.

[8] Statement of the Canadian Hierarchy, *Marriage and the Family*, Oct. 14 and 15, 1953.

[9] Thus, Noldin-Schmitt assert: "Familiar associations which are called company-keeping *per se* contain an occasion of sin. . . . If they take place in view of marriage they are lawful. . . . But care must be taken lest lawful meetings become a proximate occasion of sin." (*Op. cit.*, III, n. 419).

[10] *American Weekly*, April 18, 1954, p. 6.

[11] Noldin-Schmitt, *op. cit.*, n. 419.

[12] Aertnys-Damen, *op. cit.*, II, n. 523.

[13] Wouters, *Manuale theologiae moralis* (Bruges, 1933), II, n. 468.

[14] Noldin-Shmitt, *op. cit.*, III, n. 420.

[15] Canon 1061; Cf. *AER*, CXXII, 4 (April, 1950), p. 312.

[16] Cf. Merkelbach, B., *Summa theologiae moralis* (Paris, 1938), I, n. 177.

[17] *Praxis confessarii*, n. 65. (*Theologia moralis* [Rome, 1912], IV, p. 562.)

[18] "The Shame of America," *Saturday Evening Post*, Jan. 15, 1955, p. 73.

[19] *Our Sunday Visitor*, June 27, 1954.